Radical Nomad

Great Barrington Books

∾An imprint edited by Charles Lemert ∾

Keeping Good Time: Reflections on Knowledge,
Power, and People
by Avery F. Gordon (2004)

Going Down for Air: A Memoir in Search of a Subject
by Derek Sayer (2004)

The Souls of Black Folk, 100th Anniversary Edition
by W. E. B. Du Bois, with commentaries by Manning Marable,
Charles Lemert, and Cheryl Townsend Gilkes (2004)

Sociology After the Crisis, Updated Edition
by Charles Lemert (2004)

Subject to Ourselves
by Anthony Elliot (2004)

The Protestant Ethic Turns 100:
Essays on the Centenary of the Weber Thesis
edited by William H. Swatos, Jr., and Lutz Kaelber (2005)

Postmodernism Is Not What You Think
by Charles Lemert (2005)

Discourses on Liberation: An Anatomy of Critical Theory
by Kyung-Man Kim (2005)

Seeing Sociologically: The Routine Grounds of Social Action
by Harold Garfinkel, edited and introduced
by Anne Warfield Rawls (2005)

The Souls of W. E. B. Du Bois
by Alford A. Young, Jr., Manning Marable,
Elizabeth Higginbotham, Charles Lemert, and
Jerry G. Watts (2006)

Radical Nomad: C. Wright Mills and His Times
by Tom Hayden with Contemporary Reflections by
Stanley Aronowitz, Richard Flacks, and Charles Lemert (2006)

Critique for What? Cultural Studies, American Studies, Left Studies
by Joel Pfister (2006)

Everyday Life and the State
by Peter Bratsis (2006)

Thinking the Unthinkable:
An Introduction to Social Theories
by Charles Lemert (2007)

Radical Nomad
C. Wright Mills and His Times

by Tom Hayden

*Contemporary Reflections by Dick Flacks,
Stanley Aronowitz, and Charles Lemert*

Paradigm Publishers
Boulder • London

Copyright © 2006 by Paradigm Publishers

Published in the United States by Paradigm Publishers, 3360 Mitchell Lane, Suite E, Boulder, Colorado 80301 USA.

Paradigm Publishers is the trade name of Birkenkamp & Company, LLC, Dean Birkenkamp, President and Publisher.

Library of Congress Cataloging-in-Publication Data

Hayden, Tom.
    Radical nomad : C. Wright Mills and his times / Tom Hayden ; with contemporary reflection by Stanley Aronowitz, Richard Flacks, and Charles Lemert.
    p. cm.
    Includes bibliographical references and index.
    ISBN-13: 978-1-59451-201-8 (hc 13)
    ISBN-10: 1-59451-201-9 (hc 10)
    ISBN-13: 978-1-59451-202-5 (pbk 13)
    ISBN-10: 1-59451-202-7 (pbk 10)
    1. Mills, C. Wright (Charles Wright), 1916-1962—Political and social views.
2. Mills, C. Wright (Charles Wright), 1916-1962—Influence.   3. Radicalism—
United States.   4. New Left—United States.   5. Sociology.   6. United States—
Social conditions—1945- I. Aronowitz, Stanley.   II. Flacks, Richard.   III. Lemert,
Charles C., 1937- IV. Title.
    HM479.M55H39 2006
    301.092—dc22

                                                                    2006001599

Printed and bound in the United States of America on acid-free paper that meets the standards of the American National Standard for Permanence of Paper for Printed Library Materials.

Designed and Typeset by Straight Creek Bookmakers.

10 09 08 07 06
5 4 3 2 1

Contents

C. Wright Mills, Tom Hayden, and the New Left

Dick Flacks

Tom Hayden wrote his M.A. thesis while he was intensely engaged in the leadership of the early sixties New Left. He wrote it after returning to graduate school in Ann Arbor, having graduated from Michigan in 1961.

Hayden, at age twenty-two, was already a prime mover in the creation of the sixties. In the summer of 1960, as the newly appointed editor in chief of the *Michigan Daily,* he traveled to California to witness the emerging student movement in Berkeley, the beginnings of farmworker organizing in the California fields, and the nomination of JFK at the Democratic convention in LA (where he interviewed Martin Luther King as he picketed the convention arena). In his year as student editor, Hayden traveled in the South, documenting and helping the rising southern student movement. He wrote long, prescient articles describing and helping define what he saw as an authentic new student movement.

After graduating, Hayden decided to commit himself to that movement as an activist and as a writer. He traveled in the South, getting to know the young civil rights leadership, getting beaten in Mississippi, getting married to an eloquent and beautiful white Texas civil rights activist, Sandra Cason ("Casey"). At the same time, he agreed to join Al Haber and other Ann Arborites to help launch Students for a Democratic Society (SDS), a national organization aimed at fostering the new movement. His first big job for SDS was to draft a manifesto to be debated at the SDS founding meeting at Port Huron, Michigan, in June. The Port Huron Statement is acknowledged to be the foundational document of the New Left in the United States.

Hayden was elected SDS president at that Port Huron meeting and decided to come back to Ann Arbor with Casey Hayden to establish an SDS office there, while enrolling in the political science graduate program. I don't know whether any of the political science faculty had reservations about Hayden's capacity to complete an M.A. while indefatigably organizing, traveling, speaking, and writing on behalf of the movement. I imagine that any reservations were balanced by the obvious fact that this twenty-two-year-old was so brilliant, so intense, and so promising that he deserved to be supported. The book-length master's thesis that he produced certainly validated the decision to admit him.[1]

We need to read the work in its historical context in order to understand Hayden's angle of vision. It was being composed in the heat of the southern movement and while its author was actively engaged in efforts to inspire a burgeoning white student movement that would extend the potentials of the southern student uprising. It was a time when established understandings about the stability of the social order were crumbling—and when socially conscious young people were feeling hope about both the social future and their own potential for affecting it.

Keep in mind as well that this essay was written before the major shaping events that now define the sixties for us: before the Berkeley free speech movement (or any other sign of the possibility that *masses* of white students would take action), before Vietnam, before the ghetto uprisings. It captures reflections appropriate to a particular moment in a time of tumultuous change. Given that, I was surprised, in rereading it, by how valuable it continues to be forty years later.

Mills's New Left

C. Wright Mills was hungry for a new Left long before the sixties. By the 1950s, he was openly, angrily critical of the old Left—not just the Marxist/Trotskyist sectarian Left that many of his generation disdained, but the broader liberal Left that he saw as exhausted programmatically and accommodating to the cold war consensus in many ways. In pamphlets and articles written in the late 1950s, we see him arguing for organized and strategic dissent based on new social understandings, language, and agency. More than any other figure in the U.S. political/intellectual scene, he was trying, in the peak cold war time, to foster the possibility for a new Left not only by seeking it but by trying to constitute its intellectual foundations.

Mills's intellectual development was itself a synthesis of many of the strands of critical theory and radical tradition that became the defining features of the New Left project. He was schooled in the pragmatism of Mead and Dewey and in the critical theory of the Frankfurt School and other European Marxists. His social worlds spanned both the academy and the circles of labor and socialist intellectuals. In the space of some seven years, Mills wrote a series of books and articles that contributed much to setting the agenda of what became the New Left formation in the United States. These included the *Power Elite,* an effort to rework radical analysis of power relations; a reader on Marxism with his own theoretical annotations; *The Sociological Imagination,* a scathing critique of academic sociology combined with a stirring program for its renovation; pamphleteering analysis and denunciation of the cold war and its politics; and a "Letter to the New Left" enunciating a hope for new sources of radical political agency.

A number of us who came together in Port Huron were already avid readers of these writings, either because of or in spite of our college and graduate school curricula. But Mills's appeal was not just based on his ideas. His language was refreshingly free of the jargons of the established Lefts and of the academy as well. His much-publicized "style" of writing and living was deliberately "muscular" and, I thought, "American." He was in the university (in fact, at Columbia—the leading sociology department), but he was not of it, being bitingly critical of the academic mainstream and strikingly different in pose and practice from your typical professor. So his persona itself was very appealing to student intellectuals of the time, who ourselves hoped to be in the university while rebelling against the merely academic. He was a card-carrying member of democratic leftist circles, such as the network around *Dissent* magazine, but he avidly challenged their preoccupation with anticommunism and their inability to see the new possibilities in Cuban Revolution and other stirrings in the third world. Thus, practically alone among established Left intellectuals, Mills articulated and legitimated much of the sensibility that was embodied in the early SDS group and others in the New Left.[2]

Mills's political youth was in the late 1930s and during World War II. He was of that generation of post-1930s young intellectuals who had experienced the collapse of the left upsurge in the aftermath of the Nazi-Soviet pact and the wartime consolidation of U.S. society. These events were particularly traumatic for left-wing college students of the late 1930s, who had witnessed the disintegration of the promising American Student Union in which young communists and socialists had managed to sustain an alliance, which was torn apart because of the Hitler–Stalin pact and the bitter factionalisms that arose after that. This betrayal was followed by the readiness of left-wing labor leaders to become full partners in the war mobilization (enforcing a no-strike pledge).

Quite a few young socialists of that generation became sociologists. If the point had been to change the world, this cohort came to see that understanding had to take priority.

Mills was a member of this age cohort but hadn't had the political involvements of some of his peers. Unlike many of them, he seemed determined from the outset to be a sociologist rather than a labor organizer or a revolutionary. But I situate him in this cohort because, like the rest, he saw sociology as the foundation for fundamental revision of the orthodox Marxism that had been the intellectual resource for all of the 1930s Left factions. He shared with the ex-Trotskyists and ex-YPSLs (members of the Young People's Socialist League) of his age group a perception that the theoretical foundations of left-wing politics had to be fundamentally revised if there was to be a viable left in the United States.[3]

Mills as Revisionist

The central revision had to do with class. A united and class-conscious proletariat seemed possible in the Depression-era 1930s, but the postwar boom, and the trajectory of the labor movement in its context, called all that into question. At least three key ideas were shared by virtually all post-Marxist social critics in the 1950s: (1) that the working class was not unified structurally because of the rise of the white-collar labor force; (2) that its members were attracted to opportunities for a better life made available by consumer capitalism rather than by the prospects provided by class struggle; and (3) that the capitalist state was capable of adapting to and overcoming economic crisis (and corporations were becoming ready for such an interventionist state) through welfare state, Keynesian policies. These perceptions led to a conclusion that is embodied in virtually all social criticism written in the 1950s: *Mass-mediated consumer society was fundamentally undermining both Marxist and liberal hopes for democratic political action by ordinary people.*

Most of those who were constructing this analysis had grounds for celebration in this situation: Working people could have decent living standards and expect their children to have the opportunity for better lives not because of inherited property and privilege but as a result of their own achievement in education and career. Capitalism's costs could be controlled by policy and routine politics allowing the state to be the great social balancer. There was no longer a need for class polarization and bitter conflict to produce progressive reform.

Some ex-socialist social analysts embraced a manifestly conservative perspective, declaring that democratic hope had always been an illusion, and that the good news of the postwar society was that an elite of professional managers, experts, and public officials could use tested, "scientific" knowledge to solve social problems rather than rely on the easily manipulated enthusiasms of popular opinion and mass movements. The new postwar conservative tone was buttressed of course by the shared belief that the United States was far more progressive, democratic, and egalitarian than the totalitarian states with whom it was competing and struggling against.

Mills accepted the main lines of the postwar analysis described here, but he stood out by refusing to celebrate it. His principal worry was the international situation—the nuclear balance of terror—and the frightening risks and waste that this entailed were far more preoccupying than domestic conditions. As Tom Hayden suggests, Mills devoted little attention to the ugliness of McCarthyism—he seemed willing to believe that this was the product of marginal right-wing mobilizations rather than inherent in the "main drift." And, like most 1950s intellectuals, he seemed to regard poverty and racial inequality as residual social problems that would naturally be reduced by the logic of the welfare state.[4]

In contrast, Mills saw the arms race as an inherent feature of the postwar system; he believed that it would inevitably spiral out of control, while the Americans were being transformed at their peril into a mass of "cheerful robots." His nightmare imagery is that of a society dominated by an irrational and unaccountable elite, leading a vast population unable to know or express their interests toward war and/or a kind of dictatorship.

Mills saw only one real hope for changing this dynamic: the emergence of a stratum of intellectuals (teachers, preachers, writers, artists, other professionals, etc.) who could articulate new moral and political grounds for opposition. His last years were focused on imagining a force that would reach the elite and penetrate mass media. He imagined, in other words, that a new Left, largely constituted by intellectuals, was on the immediate horizon.

What Mills Got Wrong

One of the virtues of Marxism as a social theory is that it makes predictions about societal-level tendencies and outcomes. These predictions are derived from a detailed underlying social analysis. If predictions made in this way don't materialize, we are compelled to scrutinize that underlying analysis to find out where it went wrong. Accordingly, we can learn more from failures of social prediction than from their realization. Much of the research and theory that constitute twentieth-century social psychology and sociology began with efforts to answer such questions as "Where did Marx go wrong?" and "Why is there no socialist movement in the United States?"

Mills, like others of his generation of social scientists, was driven to understand why the left of the 1930s had declined. We can read virtually all of his work in the fifties as efforts to test and challenge the expectations and predictions of that left and to examine American social reality, especially realities of class structure, in light of the failures of orthodox Marxian class analysis and socialist hopes.

Mills preferred to say that he was diagnosing the "main drift" in society rather than claiming to be making predictions. Hayden, in *Radical Nomad,* turns the tables on Mills. The social reality

Hayden was experiencing was falsifying Mills's depiction of the main drift. Seeing how Mills went wrong might help provide the foundation for a usable social analysis for the sixties.

The most important thing that Mills missed was the civil rights movement. I don't think Mills in all his work takes account of racial oppression as a fundamental structural fact. In any case, the idea that American Negroes might become the prime agency of change was not a plausible expectation given his understanding of the main drift. Fifties-era assumptions, including those of Mills, about mass society, apathy, and conformity were fundamentally challenged by the emergence of the civil rights movement. For the civil rights upsurge forced the recognition that considerable portions of the population had not been integrated into the postwar prosperity, and they were not likely to be integrated if existing power relations remained in place. The emergence of the civil rights movement showed that "mass society" had not obliterated the possibility for collective action and new consciousness to emerge in disadvantaged and subordinated sectors.

Hayden argues that this upsurge resulted not only from the historic exclusion of African Americans through institutions of segregation and discrimination, but from the continued and inherent failure of the economy to achieve full employment, urban reconstruction, and an end to poverty The prevailing postwar assumption, shared across the political spectrum, was that poverty was a residual phenomenon in advanced, welfare state capitalism. By 1964, this argument was being called into deep question. Michael Harrington's *Other America* helped revive the idea that poverty was a fundamental structural failure of capitalism. President Lyndon Johnson's announcement of a War on Poverty (and all of the public spotlighting of the poverty question that resulted) validated this argument.

That Mills doesn't refer to the civil rights movement in any of his writings seems in retrospect to suggest a major default, as Hayden makes clear. In the 1940s and 1950s, such failures of perception were typical in analysis of what was then called "race relations." Even Gunnar Myrdal's monumental study of the

American Negro assumed that the impetus to change would come from the contradictions for white Americans of the "American dilemma" rather than the collective action of Negroes. But Mills's failure to see the potential for such movement becomes harder to fathom by the early sixties when he was so eagerly searching for agencies of change—and when civil rights protest was under way. As Hayden points out, Mills passionately engaged with the Cuban Revolution but not with the simultaneous emergence of a mass movement in the U.S. South.

Hayden criticizes Mills as well for his too-ready abandonment of class analysis and political economy in his theorizing of American power structure. One of Mills's key revisions of class analysis was his emphasis on the military as an emerging center of elite power in the United States distinct from the power available to corporate elites. Hayden argues that Mills's emphasis on the independence of military, economic, and political elites understated the degree to which the preservation of corporate capitalism constitutes the main agenda for the state. It's important to acknowledge that Mills's foregrounding of the rising power of the national security bureaucracy was a crucial contribution (echoed by Eisenhower's farewell warnings about the "military industrial complex"). Still, Hayden's effort to find coherent interconnections and contradictions between economic and military power was theoretically and practically richer than Mills's mid-fifties emphasis on their analytic independence.

Despite these deep flaws in theory and observation, Mills's depiction of the shared power and perspective of the power elite remained central to Hayden's understanding of the dynamics of power. Mills emphasized that the power elite had achieved the capability to administer and steer the economy and therefore to adapt to and overcome economic crises that threatened to undermine social stability. The contradictions and crises that Marx had identified in the nineteenth century as fundamental to capitalism and as the seeds of its undoing were, in this view, made obsolete by the powers and ideology now available to the capitalist state.

The black revolt suggested that social initiative was not under the total control of the power elite. Both Presidents Kennedy and Johnson had tried to control the civil rights movement with quite limited success. On the other hand, their efforts at such management confirmed a central point of the power elite model: we are at a point in the development of formally democratic society where national elites had the means and the will to take control of the direction of history. Elite reaction to the black revolt indicated that, when such control was threatened, there would be strong tendencies within the elite to adapt to unexpected change (rather than suppress it) in order to restore their power and legitimacy.

In *Radical Nomad,* Hayden suggests that the main effect of grassroots protest in contemporary society is to compel such elite adaptation. The most likely positive result of social movements is to force state and corporate elites to undertake reform in order to save the system. Like the New Deal's relation to labor revolt, LBJ's War on Poverty was strong evidence for the proposition that rising black protest provided the rationale for Kennedy and Johnson to push for reforms that were not previously on the elite agenda. Indeed, Hayden writes as if he expects that a likely outcome of the civil rights movement would be a further consolidation of elite control because of the integrative effects of political and economic reforms that could be expected to be sponsored from above.

This argument was not made cynically. On the contrary, Hayden saw the possibility that elite steering of reform might encourage a continuing explosion of grassroots movement (on both the left and right) and, therefore, a growing potential for reform policies and leadership that would go beyond the "aggressive tokenism" of the corporate state. Reform-minded elites will need the support of reform-hungry movements; such alliances provide intellectual and political opportunities for more far-reaching democratic change than the elites themselves may contemplate.

Read the final pages of *Radical Nomad,* and I think you'll be struck with how prescient much of its analysis was. Hayden anticipated the hunger for reform that fueled the explosion of social movements in the decade that followed. He saw new opportunities for organized liberalism (the national alliance of labor, established civil rights, and liberal organizations) but wondered, presciently, whether its leadership had the will to seize them. He foresaw the rise of a grassroots right wing in reaction to the civil rights movement and other change, but, not so presciently, he assumed that its political effect would be marginal, because of the control that would be exercised by the more rational, centrist power elite. He was, as we might expect, romantically optimistic about the rise of a new generation of radical intellectuals and activists. They, he predicts, will create a new Left appropriate to the post–cold war, postscarcity era, fusing direct action with normal politics, linking politics and culture, and devising the means for "reaching all the people" and "taking power."

What Hayden was able to foresee, then, was the potential for far-reaching movement from below in a society that had been depicted by mainstream social science as well as by Mills as largely stabilized and manipulated from above. I think he was able to see that because of his activist standpoint derived from a passionate commitment to fostering the movement he was predicting. It was a standpoint that was missing from all the social science one could then read in school, including Mills. The failure of academic social science to grasp the social change potentials of the time was itself an important spur to New Left rebellion. Many of us who gathered at Port Huron shared with Hayden a confidence that we understood the main drift better than our teachers.

That confidence was, I think, justified. Separation of academic sociologists from activist experience tends to incapacitate them as analysts of emergent social movements.[5] Those of us who were striving to be activist intellectuals were, I think, able to see empirical realities that validated our romantic hopes. But all of us who have lived through the following decades as activist intellectuals know that our own understandings, presuppositions, and expectations were themselves falsified by the actual history of our time.

I want to highlight here two major failures:

- The unanticipated decline of the power elite
- The decline of the New Left

Regarding the first point, the unanticipated decline of the power elite, Mills thought that the power elite were guilty of a "higher irresponsibility"; he characterized their policies as "crackpot realism." Such invectives referred to the commitment of elites to the nuclear arms race and the cold war—a commitment that seemed quite likely to end in the obliteration of the human race. On the other hand, Mills depicted the elite circle as led by men who wanted to rule the society in terms of a shared definition of the national interest. Their rationality might be limited, but a modicum of elite reason had to be granted. Tom Hayden, and other New Left intellectuals, assumed this even more than Mills did. So, for example, we expected that key members of the power elite would endorse or concede reforms because of their shared rationality. New Left historians coined the term *corporate liberalism* as a way of conceptualizing this sense of the dominant ruling circle. When we spoke of an "Establishment," we were expressing our assumption that the national ruling elite was guided by a commitment to collectively run the *system* as well as pursue their own particular interests.

The idea that there was such a permanent Establishment made up of an adaptive, relatively rational governing elite started to lose its relevance about twenty-five years ago. Probably beginning in the Reagan years, the shared elite commitment to governance has been replaced by much narrower and more self-serving modes of operation. The current Bush regime culminates a long period in which the managerial ethos of the corporate elite has given way to personal greed; system-maintaining perspectives in the policymaking arena have lost out to "ideas" designed to further narrow class interest; sophisticated ideologies of technocratic and administrative planning have been marginalized by free market utopianism (used to cloak greed and privilege); and meritocratic claims have lost out to cronyism. Both Mills and Hayden, like most social observers, overestimated the capacity and will of the power elite actually to take responsibility for the system. And virtually no one, prior to the 1980s, anticipated that free market ideology would replace the long-standing hegemony of corporate liberalism.

Assuming that this description is an apt characterization of a fundamental shift in the workings of national power, how can we account for this state of affairs? One critical fact is that "globalization" has undermined the willingness and ability of national elites to use the tools of economic steering that Keynesian/welfare state policies had provided in the postwar world. The emergence of a transnational economic system has hollowed out the capacities of national states to promote reform as a way of alleviating mass discontent. And the globalization of investment markets has focused managers on short-run profit maximization rather than longer-term planning perspectives. Those elite figures who continue to talk about system maintenance and the long term are now often labeled as marginal, and even radical, figures (consider George Soros and Felix Rohatyn as two examples).

Mills's mapping of the power elite stimulated a large body of academic research (the work of William Domhoff was seminal) and journalistic muckraking. By the mid-1970s, a sociology of the state was in full swing; much was mapped and theorized. We need an examination of the failure of that entire intellectual enterprise to anticipate the transformation of the national state and national politics in the era of globalization, as part of the general effort to construct a theory of power appropriate to this era.

Now let's consider the second point, the decline of the New Left. In 1964, Tom Hayden exclaimed that, had Mills lived, he would have been excited by the degree to which the new left had already far surpassed Mills's early 1960s expectations. No longer was it just an intellectual current being made by a few writers in England, Europe, and maybe the USSR. No longer was the Cuban Revolution needed as the main embodiment of the hopes and fantasies of some of these left-wing intellectuals. In the United States, a mass of students—black and white—were its embodiment, and these individuals were soon to be joined by counterparts in Germany, France, Italy, and globally. Mills had feared the coming of a mass of "cheerful robots." The rise of a mass New Left, and the broader youth revolt, suggested potentials for personal and collective resistance that he had not hoped possible.

What happened to that formation? For those of us who are veterans of the New Left, the question of what happened to it is much like the thirties generation's questions about their own political failure, and indeed like the questions asked by Werner Sombart at the beginning of the twentieth century ("Why no socialism in America?") or by the Frankfurt School after the rise of Hitler. Yet despite the vast literature on the sixties, a shared and satisfying analysis has yet to be produced. Indeed, it isn't even certain what the right questions are.

In the early sixties, a coherent New Left was coming into being. It was prefigured by the writing of Mills and a handful of other radical intellectuals such as Paul Goodman, A. J. Muste, I. F. Stone, Harvey Swados, William Appleman Williams, and members of the self-proclaimed New Left in Britain. A number of remarkable little political magazines sprouted at various universities in the first years of the sixties. The southern student sit-ins sparked a growing wave of student activism on northern campuses, not only in support of the southern movement but in opposition to nuclear testing and the House Un-American Activities Committee. The formation of SDS and the release of its Port Huron Statement in 1962 made it clear that an American New Left was now an organized force.

The early New Left's coherence depended to a considerable degree on its diagnosis of political possibility. SDSers expected that a new liberal-labor political coalition would crystallize whose aim would be to transform the Democratic Party into an authentically progressive force. As young activists, we expected the leadership for such an effort to come from our elders; our role was to support the direct action and grassroots movement that would create the pressure and space for electoral and legislative reform. The early New Left's focus on a domestic program and organizing in poor communities made strategic sense in the context of this expected new liberal political thrust.

One could remain optimistic about this possibility even after the trauma of President Kennedy's assassination. Johnson's first months as president were marked by the greatest period of legislative reform since the thirties. The War on Poverty, Medicare, federal aid to education, and other Great Society initiatives validated SDS's analysis of the main drift. Some of the design of the War on Poverty (i.e., to provide federal funding for community organizing to facilitate the direct participation of poor people in local decision making) was borrowed from the experiments made by SDS and others in urban neighborhood organizing. Meanwhile, initiatives were beginning in the labor movement and in the liberal religious world that were promising new strategies for linking direct action and conventional politics.

This promising moment was overshadowed by disillusioning frustration. Liberal and labor national leadership compromised the dramatic struggle of the Mississippi Freedom Democrats rather than, as SNCC and SDS had hoped, using that struggle as a lever for defeating Dixiecrat power in the Democratic Party. Then, as the Johnson administration escalated the Vietnam War, most of that liberal leadership went along, with union leaders among the staunchest of Johnson's pillars. Vietnam destroyed the national liberal coalition even as it fueled the mass movement of radicalizing youth.

Meanwhile, the black revolt became an urban struggle for economic as well as racial justice. Young new leftists increasingly came to see that revolt as the spearhead of social change. Strategies based on legislated reform and electoral power appeared to have failed; emotion, language, and action were, by the end of the 1960s, framed by a rhetoric of "revolution." This stance meant the abandonment of the Port Huron Statement's "reformist" perspective and its replacement by various mélanges of Mao, Che, and Malcolm. The late sixties New Left defined itself in resistance to

American imperialism, rather than as a force that could connect with an American majority. This fundamental shift in groups such as SDS happened not only because of changes in its leadership personnel but also because of changes in the hearts and minds of many, including Tom Hayden, who had helped create the early New Left. And, in 1968, 1969, and 1970, as mass uprisings met by official violence seemed to spread across the planet, apocalyptic expectations were hard to avoid on every side.

By the early seventies, apocalyptic visions and revolutionary rhetoric came to seem delusory. New Leftists realized the need to find long-term political vocation. There was a return to electoral activity (sparked by the McGovern campaign) coupled with an effort to become geographically and institutionally rooted. Contrary to conventional wisdom, the seventies turned out to be a remarkably creative time for both organizing and politically oriented intellectual work. That was the moment when "new social movements" flowered in Europe and the United States, very much in continuity with the early New Left. At the same time, in universities and in independent think tanks, visions and programs aimed at "economic democracy," "Euro socialism," and "green" politics were being articulated, while new theoretical initiatives in all of the social sciences aimed at revising both the established disciplines and the Marxist legacy. Tom Hayden himself ran for the U.S. Senate in the California Democratic primary in 1976 (and amassed a million votes). He based his candidacy on a vision of "economic democracy" that was spelled out in a lengthy campaign document whose roots in the Port Huron Statement were hardly accidental.

I think in a number of ways the New Left as a style of thought and as a loose social network really began to come into its own in the political and intellectual projects of the seventies, many of which tried to synthesize emphasis on radical democracy with feminist, ecological, and socialist perspectives.

The seventies New Left tended to return to early sixties expectations about the main drift: the hope that out of the local organizing, new social movements, and new visions of reform, there would be a revival of the national liberal coalition that would, finally, be sufficiently determined and unified to seek power in the Democratic Party. Such hopes failed to take account of the collapse of corporate liberalism and the rise of an aggressive, strategically insightful New Right, financed by significant numbers of the corporate elite. Reagan's election in 1980 would have been unimaginable ten years earlier; and, of course, that election signaled a fundamental turning point in national politics.

For veterans of the sixties, the growing national power of the Right led to an increasingly defensive political posture. Visions of fundamental reform were largely abandoned as liberal and leftist leaders, activists, and intellectuals have tried to defend the safety nets, social wages, and civil rights that many of us had come to take for granted and had previously criticized for their token character.

Still, despite the stagnation of progressive politics on a national level, the New Left as a perspective and style of doing politics continues. The global activism represented by the movement for global justice has some of its roots in the sixties movements and shares much of its spirit: decentered structures, bottom-up decision making, efforts to create new vision and resist doctrinal thinking, and a preference for direct action rather than administered politics. Tom Hayden has returned to his movement-organizing mode, as a leader in antisweatshop activism, as a witness in Chiapas and Porto Allegre, and as an active opponent to the Iraq war. Many of those who were at Port Huron have been similarly engaged. In a variety of geographic and institutional locales, sixties veterans have become the elders and mentors of succeeding generations of activists.

I think one thing our experience over the last four decades makes clear is that it is much harder than we thought to anticipate the "main drift." We're a political generation whose beliefs about what was coming next have, at every turn, been falsified by events. As I've been saying here, you can learn a lot by examining such errors of prediction. I suspect, though, that much of the time we have preferred to move on rather than fully analyze where we went wrong. In this, New Left veterans are hardly alone: the inventory of failed expectations spans the whole political spectrum and most of the leading theoretical constructions of the last forty years.

That theoretically derived expectations about the political future fail is inevitable. Human actors can remake history in defiance of what everyone knows to be the main drift. And the multilayered complexity of contemporary society can never be adequately theorized. But, as I have been trying to suggest here, the failure of social theory enhances knowledge, provided we try to examine deeply what theory failed to take into account, what potentials it ignored, what assumptions were too simple. That's what Mills did to Marxism, what Hayden did to Mills, and what a new generation needs to do to the theory that the New Left embodied.

Notes

1. Tom Hayden tells his story in *Reunion: A Memoir* (New York: Collier Books, 1989); the creation of SDS and the Port Huron Statement is detailed in James Miller, *"Democracy Is in the Streets": From Port Huron to the Streets of Chicago* (New York: Simon & Schuster, 1987). Some of what I write here is based on my personal relationship with Hayden and my involvement with the SDS founding and the writing of the Port Huron Statement.

2. Mills was by no means the only American intellectual who influenced and expressed that sensibility. But others—notably, Paul Goodman, Dwight MacDonald, Paul Sweezy, A. J. Muste, and W. E. B. Du Bois—were outside the academy and therefore less able to *legitimate* radical critique.

3. Biographical materials on Mills are available in C. Wright Mills, *Letters and Autobiographical Writings,* ed. Kathryn Mills with Pamela Mills (Berkeley: University of California Press, 2000).

4. See Maurice Isserman, *If I Had a Hammer: The Death of the Old Left and the Birth of the New Left* (Urbana: University of Illinois Press,

1993); Peter Clecak, *Radical Paradoxes: Dilemmas of the American Left, 1945–1970* (New York: Harper & Row, 1973).

5. I've spelled out this argument in Richard Flacks, "Knowledge for What? Thoughts on the State of Social Movements Studies," in *Rethinking Social Movements: Structure, Meaning, and Emotion,* ed. Jeff Goodwin and James M. Jasper (Lanham, Md.: Rowman & Littlefield, 2004), chap. 10.

On Tom Hayden's
Radical Nomad

Stanley Aronowitz

For me, spring 1962 was an eventful time. It was the year of the Cuba Missile Crisis, which reminded us all that our worst fears were by no means a case of paranoia. In March, after surviving several heart attacks and a lifetime of frenetic living, C. Wright Mills died. I was the campaign manager of Democratic Assembly member Mark Lane's unsuccessful bid to become the Democratic Reform movement's candidate for the Nineteenth Congressional District seat that swung around Manhattan like a bell curve. I left Newark and separated from my wife, with whom I had lived for ten years, and through a new romantic friendship I met Tom and Casey Hayden, Al Haber, and many of the early members of Students for a Democratic Society (SDS).

Tom, Casey, Al, and my recent friend, Evelyn Leopold, shared an apartment in West Chelsea. Of course, like most young New

York activists, they were enthusiastic about Mark's display of singular dissent from the overwhelming complacency that marked ordinary politics. He had made waves in the party establishment and headlines by exposing the commercial shenanigans that lay behind a measure, introduced in the state legislature by its Republican leadership, to build fallout shelters in every school. But then, as now, the Democrats hesitated before the wall of national security. They were shy to oppose a proposal that was paraded as a bill to safeguard New Yorkers from the threat of a probable nuclear attack perpetrated by that "terrorist" state, the Soviet Union.

I was twenty-nine, six or seven years older than the people living in the apartment. In addition to my connection with the Lane campaign, they were drawn to me because of my job as a union organizer. They were intensely interested in the labor movement because, despite their intellectual skepticism, they were still imbued with a fair dose of what C. Wright Mills called the "labor metaphysic." They were trying to assess its potential to effect "progressive" social change against the prevailing corporate-dominated power "structure." Tom was especially keen to talk because he was in the throes of writing a political statement for SDS's upcoming inaugural national conference in Port Huron, Michigan. During much of April, he interviewed me about employment, union policy, and economics. When the piece was finally written, I could see several traces of our conversations as well as footprints of Michael Harrington's current bestseller, *The Other America,* probably the most famous and influential book on poverty in the American twentieth century, and C. Wright Mills's *The Power Elite,* which I had read when it first appeared in 1956.

The Port Huron Statement is a manifesto of democratic hope combined with strong criticism of the corporate power that had come to dominate American political culture. It contains a powerful condemnation of poverty amid unprecedented postwar American affluence. And, a few years before, the Voting and Civil Rights acts—which, despite their considerable merit, left the economic oppression of blacks untouched because their promise was that political and civil rights would be enough to address the issues of racially based poverty and economic inequality—argued that the root of racism and racial discrimination lay in the structure of economic power. Most of all, it called on America to make good on its promise of equality for all and to fulfill a new participatory democracy, in which ordinary people make the decisions that affect their lives. But Hayden's tract was addressed as well to the Kennedy administration to translate its visionary rhetoric of change into concrete steps. In subsequent years, he was to have a lot to do with the Kennedys through what became the debacle of the Southeast Asia wars, of which they had been the leading protagonists.

In retrospect, one can discern the close connection between the Port Huron Statement and *Radical Nomad*. Port Huron is a document of a putative radical democratic movement yet to be born, whose principal concepts were to be shattered less than three years later by the Vietnam War—which triggered a different sort of radicalism. Many in Hayden's cohort became socialists or communists and joined the old parties. Some who came to disdain what, at the time of the Cuban Revolution and the Vietnam War, appeared as relatively moderate declarations contained in the Port Huron Statement, formed revolutionary new parties and groups, most of which ultimately failed. Tom always had an acute sense of American political reality; his ideas were critical, but his practical politics were only a few steps ahead of the prevailing situation. He joined none of the new party formations, even as his ideological politics shifted.

Sometime in 1964 or 1965, when he had moved to Newark to participate in an SDS organizing project among poor blacks in the Clinton Hill neighborhood, Tom handed me a copy of his master's thesis, "Radical Nomad." At the time I thought it an especially prodigious piece of work. What impressed me most was the crisp writing and clear exposition. Almost forty years later, I read it again. By now, in connection with a project commissioned by Sage Publishers in 2001 to collect four volumes of the best and representative ninety or so articles and reviews on Mills's work, I had read the corpus of Mills's own writings and nearly all the critics'. Of the more than four hundred articles, with barely a dozen exceptions, most writers were intellectually incapable of dealing with Mills's central thesis, and even the best often criticized Mills from unacknowledged ideological assumptions. Tom's thesis is closely reasoned and properly starts from Mills's own perspective, departing from it only when the reader understands what Mills is saying. Of course, "Radical Nomad" was too long for a collection of articles, but I believed it should be published as a short book, and I am pleased that Paradigm saw the merit of the venture.

Radical Nomad is simply the best and fullest exposition and criticism of Mills's theory of power we have. It barely addresses elements of cultural, social, and social psychological theory that preoccupied Mills at different points in his career, but it focuses sharply on what Mills says about the economic and political structure of American society. The thesis originally was written six years after the publication of the *Power Elite,* which was widely reviewed and discussed, and it continues to attract younger scholars. But in the chill to radical intellectual inquiry that marked the cold war and the hostility of its intellectual supplicants, Mills's book suffered considerable repudiation by liberal commentators, criticism by orthodox Marxists for its refusal to name a unified capitalist ruling class, and crass attacks by even some erstwhile radicals who had come to embrace the American system. It is no exaggeration to note that Hayden's analysis, written at a moment of renewed cold war hysteria, must be considered both courageous and singular.

Although Tom takes issue with some of Mills's formulations, particularly the prominence Mills accords to the military in the constitution of power, and the absence of a treatment of race, the book aligns itself with the central proposition of Mills's major work, *The Power Elite.* With Mills, he repudiates the theory of pluralism adopted by prevailing political science of the time according to which there is no hierarchy of economic and political power, only a multitude of contesting "interest groups" that, at the national and local levels, vie for power on a more or less equal playing field. He defends Mills for identifying the main lines of power in terms of specific institutional arrangements. In fact, Tom goes further than Mills. His discourse is less an analysis of alliances among the political, military, and economic elites and the individuals who constitute them that we find in Mills, than a more straightforward argument for the existence of a ruling class.

The thesis was written at the apex of the civil rights movement, ignited by Rosa Parks's refusal to move to the back of bus in Montgomery, Alabama, in 1955, which gave rise to the celebrated boycott, when thousands of black citizens walked the streets rather than ride in segregated public transportation, and when, beginning in 1959, lunch counter sit-ins, marches, and demonstrations electrified the country, particularly its youth. Tom takes Mills to task for failing to address the question of race discrimination and racial oppression either in his narratives of power or anywhere else. But the evidence presented in a collection of his letters and autobiographical writings indicates that Mills was aware of these issues, but, in his own words, "I have never been interested in what is called 'the Negro Problem.' Perhaps I should have been and should now." [1] His failure, perhaps refusal, to address them within the scope of his theory of power in America is, to say the least, puzzling, even though he says clearly that he abhors racism. I think it is a fair conjecture to say that he thought race and gender discrimination, however atrocious (indeed, he offers an anecdote from his own experience that illustrates his view that race is a "white" problem), were derivative of class and stratification, a function of power relations.

Tom Hayden went on to win elective office in California and play a significant role in that state's legislature on behalf of progressive legislation. But he shares with Mills the position of public intellectual. Whether as a student leader, community organizer, or politician, he has remained a prolific and compelling writer, a tribune of sometimes-unpopular political causes, a controversial figure on the left, and one of the best public speakers I have heard. Through the years, I have read with pleasure his books on contemporary politics, and I am particularly fond of the book in which he rediscovers his own Irish heritage. *Radical Nomad* reveals a different side: here is a theoretically sophisticated thinker whose style never wavers from an intention to reach beyond the university environment in which he was nurtured, to a wider public. After more than forty years, at a moment when most intellectuals in and out of the academy have abdicated their responsibility to speak about the concentration of political and economic power, or are content to nibble at the edges of the crisis of our time rather than naming the system that has produced it, this book remains a shining example of political analysis as it should be made. It is as relevant today as when it was written.

Note

1. C. Wright Mills, *Letters and Autobiographical Writings*, ed. Kathryn Mills with Pamela Mills (Berkeley: University of California Press, 2000), 314.

After Mills: 1962 and Bad Dreams of Good Times

Charles Lemert

WHEN TOM HAYDEN AWOKE THAT MORNING IN THE SPRING of 1962 to news of the death of C. Wright Mills, he awoke, as did many of us, to changes in the world order that few, if any, understood were coming. He awoke having just completed a draft of the Port Huron Statement, one of the documents that would wake the world. Those who were then young enough to march in the revolutionary 1960s were beginning their time just when Mills ended his. Time plays tricks of this sort. A death can clear the decks for a new beginning. Theatrically, such an ending is usually that of an evil hand who held a power that held back the floods. Though Mills had his detractors who may have rejoiced at this passing, the tide he helped conjure up was already turning for the good, or so it seemed.

Occasionally the fall of a good man can open the gates for a sea change. The year following, late August, W. E. B. Du Bois died in Ghana the night before Martin Luther King's dream speech at the March on Washington—leaving open the question: If Du Bois had survived and deigned to return to the United States to speak, would his very presence have altered the political circumstances that produced the long enduring legislative gains of the short-lived American civil rights movement? Surely Du Bois would never have obeyed the Kennedy administration's prohibitions on revolutionary talk in the most precious of national parks. His presence in Washington on August 28, 1963, might well have hastened the already-gathering storm of black power that, after 1965, would spell the end of integrationist dreams of racial hand holding. Mills, great as he was, was not a man (as he would have put it) of Du Bois's stature. This is to take nothing away from Mills. Few American radicals of that day rose to the level of Du Bois's intellectual and political importance. Still, at a crucial time, for a pivotal stratum of mostly white university students, Mills was the man who started something. Babies were named after him. Documents were composed in his spirit. Actions were taken under the banner of his ideas. He would not live to see any of it.

Hence the creepy effect of the C. Wright Mills in Tom Hayden's *Radical Nomad,* a book on Mills written as Mills would have—well parsed, vibrant, packed with fact, edgy in its own way, critically pressed beyond its subject. Written in the early years of the student movement Mills influenced, the manuscript had been forgotten since 1964—ignored, if not forgotten, even by its author and others who had read it then. To read *Radical Nomad* so long after Mills was buried is to exhume the bones of hope for the genetic code to a moment in history when the worlds we now must face were conceived to gestate in a fibroid womb.

We who are old enough to tell stories of these times past are likely to be surprised by the C. Wright Mills encoded by Hayden in *Radical Nomad.* The surprise arises on the literary flare of the book that brings Mills himself back to life sufficiently well as to put the living on notice. It is shocking to realize what then we could not have anticipated—that Mills, whose work was of another time, survives in our time as the *camera obscura* of what we admired in him. Today, Mills is *more,* not less, a topic of academic discussion than in his day—a reversal of the fortune he sought. He shunned academic sociologists who shunned him, taking his case to a public that knew him well. He would have abhorred some of the distortions of what he valued. Well into the 2000s, academic sociologists carry on tirelessly about public intellectuals, speaking only to fellow academics. Some (one most notably) of Mills's closest followers seize the public eye with florid talk that betrays the political values Mills defined. Abstracted empiricists no better than the ones Mills denounced let his words spill from their tongues as they try in vain to suck up to students indifferent to the inane. At the limit of the absurd, some—who in the 1960s recused themselves to carrels to read Wittgenstein as relief from Parsons—come forth with collected essays on how the sixties affected their thinking. One can only imagine!

Reading Tom Hayden on Mills in light of his own life-long work in, if not of, American public life is refreshing beyond words; no less the essays by Dick Flacks and Stanley Aronowitz, who themselves kept their left feet in the public mess as they taught radical politics in the academy. At the same time, even so sharp an analytic presentation of Mills as Hayden's reminds just how much his Mills is a ghost of another era—an Achilles from a brutal past he slew, who, having taken an arrow from his Paris, never enjoyed the fruit of his victories. *Radical Nomad* asks the question old men and women must sooner or later consider: When, if not then, did the world we today look out upon, and are soon to leave to our heirs, begin to turn away from the values so many of us trusted?

The genius of C. Wright Mills was that he somehow managed to juggle the old and new of his day—which was, easy to forget, the day of the inglorious 1950s. He was, as Dick Flacks says, muscular—hard driven, rough, pressing, plainspoken, always cutting sharply against the grain of prevailing comforts. He was, as such men are, a fatal type, well presented. Under the sinews a tender heart beats arrhythmically. Such men can do no other. When, after the first heart attack, his doctor told him to avoid stress, Mills said, "That's like telling me to avoid eating or breathing."[1] He died still young, tender before the brutalities he brought upon himself.

So many years later we who admired him in our youth come to the time of our deaths pondering the whys and wherefores of times Mills never knew. In a way, for some at least, he helped us survive what he could not; and survive we do with questions no one but our children's children can answer. Is a weak heart a trouble or an issue? Did we, after a time, avoid stress too much, trust ourselves too little? Did we burn our own stew, choosing to stir the pot on top without tending the fires below? Did we retire too early just when today's conflagration was slowly spreading in the undergrowth our marches crushed? Do we now do enough to train and encourage the young who might take up what we put down? Was the conviction that only the young can change the world a self-justification of our generation's unacknowledged fear of the deadly worlds that killed so many we followed? Is not Mills, dead at forty-five while still living as though we were twenty-five, a specter of our own retreat? Or was his willingness to press on against the limit of his own mortality a ghost of what might have been had he not? Where are the political type-A's now that we really need them?

The people of our generation have already begun to die. We will be all but gone before our children's children are ready to take what risks they must to repair the worlds we will have left them. How do we assess what might have been had all those we admired not died young ... had we not retreated before nuclear politics now exploding ... had those who died in our youth survived? The generation of the 1960s in America was, it might be said, a virtual generation before the fact of the televisual age—a generation of young whose then-unlived future might have been other than it has become, *if only* ... Mills had not died, ... Kennedy not gone to Dallas to face the hatred of what he was becoming, ... Malcolm not gone to Mecca to learn that whites were not all devils, … Johnson not gone into Vietnam to avenge the Alamo, …Martin not gone to Memphis in the name of economic justice, …Bobby not gone to Los Angeles as the candidate of the poor,… and so on. We saw them all die. Gil Scott Heron was wrong. The revolution *was* televised, and because it was, what was achieved has been lost in the phantasmagoria of blurred images on sets with coat hanger antennas we flip on when, long before dawn, we wake from the bad dreams of what might have been.

What if, in the words Mills inspired, participatory democracy had actually overcome the fatuous rhetoric of free markets to become the true American value behind economic justice? In 1962, even as late as 1968, the dream of such a good time seemed to bring it near—ready to become. What came in its place was the vicious revenge of those who speak in words without meaning, as if to concede their nostalgia for an America that never was and never could have been—one where the men wore guns and the women believed in Jesus and minded kids who did not piss on their parade.

Some things are true and good about the generation of men and women now growing old—those who at whatever remove engaged the tumultuous decade of their youth. We were, as Mills urged, willing to imagine a different social order; and we were willing to imagine it in bold terms that struck down the pieties of our childhood—those of the labor metaphysic, of the liberal innocence before progress, of the self-righteous middle that excused violence in the name of progress, of the overwrought passions that led to a succession of Vietnams. Though the people of the passing generation were in fact bred in at least modest comfort, we at least had the courage to think against the grain of our comforts, to seek a more honest order. The single most striking aspect of the Port Huron Statement that Hayden finished the day Mills died is that it is so abrasively honest—about the world America was already shaping to the illusion of the inevitable triumph of its good people. Read it now, scrubbed of the dated references to the cold war, and it stands up very well—fresher even than the ideas Mills lent it.

The year 1962 could not have been more sadly apt to the passing away of Mills and the coming into being of the white student movement. On the surface, only the Cuban missile crisis in October, just weeks after the Port Huron meeting, stood up dramatically to the events of the year following. In periodizations of the decade, 1963 is usually, and more or less rightly, taken as the year in which the center began to lose its hold, thus opening the way for the collapse of 1968. The August 1963 March on Washington was more or less the high-water mark of the civil rights movement, after which it all turned nasty.

Though the Freedom Rides in Alabama in 1961 had been bloody (in those days, *bloody* meant "white blood"), nothing compared to Mississippi Freedom Summer of 1964 led by Bob Moses, a solitary figure from the North who braved the odds to join rural folk against their fears. That summer global attention rose in outrage at the murder of the three young civil rights men whose names thereafter are forever linked: Chaney, Goodman, and Schwerner—a black and two whites, all young. The pouring out of white blood with black in a dirt hill in rural Mississippi broke some kind of cultural barrier. Once the membrane of social separation was pierced, racial blood took on a new meaning. The exsanguinations betrayed the quasi-legal foolishness of the American race code that turned on the one-drop rule.

You would have supposed the work and pain in Mississippi might have led to a better outcome at the Democratic National Convention in Atlantic City later that summer. Instead, the hard work of Fannie Lou Hamer and the others, local and northern alike, to join the issue of black participation in the democratic process was rebuffed by Lyndon Johnson, revealing the hard Texas hand that punched up the Gulf of Tonkin Resolution, also in August 1964, which justified his full gallop into Vietnam beginning in early February 1965. The promise of Johnson's social program was soon wrecked by the cost of the war that turned progressive forces against the liberal base of northern support for civil rights. Had it not been for Selma in the spring of 1965, there might not have been a Voting Rights Act to complete the legislative gains of the 1964 Civil Rights Act (themselves a redundancy of the by-then century-old Thirteenth, Fourteenth, and Fifteenth Amendments of the U.S. Constitution).

Compared to all that transpired in the two years following, 1962 seems quiet to all but those who huddled in fear those October nights of Cuban nightmares as American forces moved at sea toward Soviet ships. Yet, when times turn against each other, they never turn on a dime. The older dispensation always hangs on, often for a good long while before the new asserts itself. In many ways, depending on the history you trust, those who lived to see the early years of the twenty-first century suffer the long-term aftereffects of moral nostalgia that would forget all that in the hair-brained scheme to restore an old American order that was never pure. At the same time, looking backward, 1962 was just as tranquil a sequel to the year of the New Frontier when so many felt the good times were really here again. John Glenn orbited the Earth. Pope John XXIII called for fresh air in the Vatican Council. Mickey Mantle was still at the top of his game. The Kennedy brothers took a step beyond their faint gestures toward blacks in the South in the 1960 election by forcing the admission of James Meredith to the University of Mississippi.

For those of us who were not children of the labor movement or of more brilliantly red diapers, these were among the events that caught our attention even before we read either C. Wright Mills or the Port Huron Statement. I for one had graduated in 1959 from a lily white public university in Ohio. Five years later, that same campus was the training ground for white students (I was not among them) preparing with black students for the movement that summer in Mississippi. Some of us were different. Tom Hayden, Dick and Mickey Flacks, and Stanley Aronowitz were among those who grew up in the older Left. Casey Hayden, who had grown up white with racial hatred in East Texas, had experienced the social injustices of the American way. Though I went to school but a few hours' drive from Ohio Wesleyan where Mary King had studied in the years before, she, too, went south to join in the struggle and, with Casey Hayden, to coauthor the now-famous and pivotal feminist text "Sex and Caste," which some consider the founding document of left feminism. In those early years when others were heeding a deeper inner voice, I—and I daresay many others like me—went through college drinking 3.2 beer and cheering Freddie Perkins on as he chased Kappas around the Sigma Chi house.

For us—we who were slow to rise to the calling—1962 was still a year of hope. The Kennedy mystique turned our heads toward politics, which was at best a dopey liberalism. "Ask not what your country can do for you ..." and all that half-baked nationalism. For the politically dim-witted, Montgomery in 1955–1956 or Little Rock in 1957 did not appear on the screen where, if the parents were out, we would watch Elvis wiggle. In the late 1950s, I was, like others, a smuggish twit cramming for medical school, calculating my grades to see if I stood a chance of beating out Stanley Nuddleman for valedictorian (as it happened some girl beat us both). It would be years before we could spell Emmett Till. Don't even mention the white Johnnies and Judies who never bothered to figure out who he was.

All this is not, however, the embarrassment you might imagine. We not of the labor metaphysic nor the white southern resistance are what we are. At the least some deep place beyond the reach of our parents and peers, somewhere under the frat boy pleasures, a light glimmered, however dimly. By 1963, I do not ever remember believing the commissioned lie that JFK was murdered by Lee Harvey Oswald alone. Even before I knew the other Marx, it seemed logical that some class or another had wanted rid of Kennedy. Even if I had not moved very far left, the speed of it all was dizzying to a kid whose only prior exposure to conspiracy theories were the invectives my parents mouthed about FDR, Walter Reuther, and the commies behind the social-ized medicine my father the doctor loathed.

1962 was somehow the year when what had long since stirred Tom Hayden and before him C. Wright Mills began to dawn on my kind of white boy. It must have been much the same instinct that touched the Kennedy brothers, turning them from the ways of their father toward a more honest liberalism. In a sense, Bobby Kennedy was made, so to speak, in 1962 in the trials with Ross Barnett and James Meredith at Mississippi. His hand was forced by the power he held, but the subsequent succession of political fools, than which none worse than Bush the younger, suggest that instincts do not always meet the demands of the world about. For many in my position, 1962 was the year we began to notice. Three years later, by then not a doctor but an ordained minister of uncertain qualifications and absurdly tepid faith, I drove all night with others behind the buses from Boston to Montgomery then on into Selma—scared shitless but determined to do whatever we were called to do. I was no longer a student. Not even close. I had quit Harvard graduate school the year before because I could no longer bear to sit on the sidelines even when I barely knew what the name of the game was.

But, then, do we ever know what the name of the game is? 1962, the year Mills died and white people started to pay attention, means nothing in itself. We mark the years according to the events as they touched us. The more touched, the more that year or some lesser date takes on meaning. The more the meaning, the more pungent the time associated with its place in social experience. Where is 9/11? It was not long a *when* so much as an entry in social space—a location in the material extension of time in relation to which people take their bearings. The day C. Wright Mills died means something to those who occupy the space he in his time helped define; just as for others the day W. E. B. Du Bois died defined the end of an era and the beginning of another, and for others November 22, 1963; and others February 21, 1965; and so on and on. When the times of those in dispersed social spaces come together, they rarely do in the case of some global event such as 9/11. More often, their movement toward each other is glacial—a slow melting of hard edges that allows the mass to budge toward the undifferentiated sea.

Such was that March morning in 1962—a decisively painful moment for Tom Hayden; a mysterious conjunctural blur waiting to happen for my kind who were already living on the fumes of our political innocence. Time, like the dates we moderns use to measure it, is never one. There are no single solitary and discrete events. Events are what events become in the recess of social time toward an end Western culture believes is the fulfillment of meaning—this against the laws of modern physics that would define a utopia as, quite literally, no place at all, a point in time where time disperses toward the flat line of maximum entropy.

Borrowing from Immanuel Wallerstein, who was taking up Fernand Braudel's social theory of time, we might suggest that there are three kinds of time[2]: the near and local time of events, the coming together of events into an unstable conjuncture, and the long-enduring time of structures. The first, event-time, is the time of local meaning; conjunctures are the clash and combination of measured local meanings; structures sediment the enduring times that come before and remain after the comings together of local happenings. Occasionally, not always, the three give off the appearance of meaningful coordination. More often they diverge along trajectories that pull at the local, shredding it into its several parts splayed in the depths of the dirt. The conjuncture is the surprising time when some shrewd and patient archaeologist uncovers just the right layer of the buried past where stuff is well settled—stuff that, on close analysis, gives meaning to the all too rapidly passing present.

Radical Nomad, the book now exhumed, has just that potential. Such a text will not, we should know, tell us a truth from a time past that will unlock the mystery of the present. Past and present are locked in the dusty embrace of structures. We come upon this book at a time in the history of our times when there is good reason to believe that the long-enduring structures of the modern age may be suffering the effects of their own flatulence—a greenhouse of foul gases hastening the global meltdown. Whatever globalization turns out to be, it will be, at the least, a time when the conjunctural histories of the old and the new, like those of the far and near and those of East and West, North and South, and so on, lost their relative tensions. In the meltdown, the dispersion of social times begins to implode. Events occur less often in a locale, more often in a global space where local and universal are one (and when they become one, they become, at best, metaphors from a former time used to discuss that which cannot be fully understood).

Reading a text like *Radical Nomad,* written in another conjuncture about a man of another time, demands unusual attentions—patience before the odd irrelevances of language and historical allusions, imagination before the possibilities of what might have been and may have become in spite of the passing of the old order. Where Mills can today be said to have failed in his day is less important than what we who read him today make of what he thought he was doing in another time—a reading that, beyond its documentary value, can have political meaning in our fast-passing present *if* we allow the discovered to measure what we did or did not do in the time Mills did not have. Hence again: An event like the death of Mills, a year like 1962, a conjunctural time like that of the 1960s, an enduring structure like that of the good half-millennium of the modern age are not so much the strain of incoherence toward a meaningful history as a clash of times (not, most certainly, of civilizations) that were once settled in far-flung places and today cannot keep themselves from joining together to kill or make love—the flatulence notwithstanding.

1962 was an event for some, a blur of a conjuncture waiting to happen for others, and business as usual for the majority, including the millions whose business was getting by on the margins. No single moment, whether that of a morning coffee in bed or that of a prolonged stress over a span of months or years, is ever an event. Events are necessarily composed after the fact in the memories social experiences produce. Events are remembered because memory produces them. Between the event and its memory very little touches down on the hard ground. C. Wright Mills could be said to have invented the American New Left in the narrow sense that, whatever it was, however ages later it is being betrayed or reconsidered, this conjuncture of white and black that rose up young to confront the old was, like all comings together in historical time, never an event, nor a structure, but a touching across differences that would soon part ways.

> We are people of this generation, bred in at least modest comfort, housed now in universities, looking uncomfortably to the world we inherit.
> —*Tom Hayden & SDS, Port Huron, Michigan, 1962*

> An organization which claims to speak for the needs of a community—as does the Student Nonviolent Coordinating Committee—must speak in the tone of that community, not as somebody else's buffer zone. This is the significance of black power as a slogan. For once, black people are going to use the words they want to use—not just the words whites want to hear.
> —*Stokely Carmichael & SNCC, Waveland, Mississippi, 1966*[3]

Racial differences aside, there could not be two more different manners of speaking—one polished by university culture, the other hardened by life on the margins. But both were set against their elders, those of another time from the one they were inventing.

If, in the bowels of that time, 1962 has a special meaning, it was the meaning of being an approximate moment when times began to separate—when the young took a stand against the world their elders had made. Yet, this stand, in the United States—at the first, one in which black and white students joined hands—was vastly more than a generational disruption. When, earlier, in December 1955 in Montgomery, Martin Luther King Jr. was anointed the leader of the bus boycott movement at the tender age of twenty-six years, he might not have risen to notice had it not been for the action of his elders—Rosa Parks who was forty-two and a seasoned civil rights worker, the older folk in the local Negro churches, most of them women who had longed for such words on the lips of an exclusively male clergy. No less, in later years, when Ella Baker held together the male ministers movement (the Southern Christian Leadership Conference [SCLC]), and when

Fannie Lou Hamer did the same for the Mississippi Freedom Party in 1964, the same year when the young white women, Casey Hayden and Mary King, stood up at Waveland to call out the men in the Student Nonviolent Coordinating Committee (SNCC). In those days in the South, the old heads were matriarchs who cooked and sewed, and risked their lives from door to door, field to field, until the men came along. When, in the years after Waveland and SNCC's split with SCLC, the emergence of the varieties of black power movements were, by then, stands against the old generation of integrationists—those who, while far from the sycophancy of Booker T. Washington, remained within the fold of accommodation to white rules of integrationist democracy. Martin Luther King was enough a genius to see the need to turn from civil to economic rights, and to know it seems that it would get him killed, as it did one spring day in 1968. Even today there are people who believe he was killed at the Lorraine Motel by someone (or someones) they called James Earl Ray. But those who in 1968 believed that had already bought a share in the bridge over troubled waters—waters that could not be calmed by homilies on human decency and such like.

In 1962, many of the white young still believed in decency—in, that is, the civility that allows civil society to thrive, a civility that is always, everywhere, defined by the mannered rules of those in charge. By 1968, those who had tried to bridge the troubles no longer believed in human decency. Too many leaders had been murdered, their deaths whitewashed by legal formalities. Too many babies had been bombed, their deaths enshrined in the platitudes of martyrdom. Too many of their colleagues had been beaten senseless, some surviving to this day with the wounds of their opposition to the righteous centerfold of America that was, by then, exposed to the prurient eyes of those willing to look at the naked truth.

Yet, even in 1968, in America and elsewhere in the northern suburbs of the European Diaspora (Berkeley, Morningside Heights, Paris, even Prague), it was very, very difficult to see the naked truth. This may be why, by the late 1960s, and especially in

America, shear nakedness became the playful rebuke of by-then tortured extensions of the platitudes Mills had so bitterly rebuked in the years before his death. Even advocates of an American New Left, and even those who had stood with black students in the South and North, were at best cautious, at times appalled, by the comic strategies of those who were associated with the so-called cultural revolution—a moniker meant for all those whose politics were insufficiently serious. Yet, by 1968 the struggle against the war in Vietnam had become the lightning rod of the once young who remained at home. We who remained at home, for whatever reason, knew very well that it was disproportionately the brothers of black brothers with whom some had marched in the South before 1966 who were dying in Vietnam. "No Viet Cong ever called me Nigger." Muhammad Ali never said those words that were first uncovered in VC propaganda spread among the mostly black American ground troops in the Mekong delta.[4] But we wanted to believe Muhammad Ali had said them, and so it was ordained. Already by 1965, Ali (just twenty-three years old, only slightly younger than Tom Hayden) was the first global political figure to make the intellectual and moral moves that had to be made if we were to understand the naked truth—Ali's prowess in sport was, and would long remain, the lesser of his transcendent brilliances. He was the first to capture the naked truth at its most lascivious. The truth of the modern West, in particular of its apotheosis in the American way, is that America was never, and never could have been, nor was it then, or is now, a social thing unto itself. America was the epitome of the modern nation-state, said to have been invented at the Peace of Westphalia in 1648 where, in fact, the nation-state came into being *only* by reason of accords that laid the structures of a global interstate system. America was no one thing. It was always a global invention such that, when it had become the most powerful nation-state, it was in fact no more than the most successful of the global colonizing nations. Everyone with eyes to see could see that the American war in Vietnam was no more, no less, than a slick form of colonizing in the name of false moral principles. "No Viet Cong ever called me

Nigger" was pure honesty—factually true but, more important, right to the ironic heart of America's global position.

As the years turned from 1962 to what Immanuel Wallerstein calls the world-revolution of 1968, what became plain is that C. Wright Mills's telling critique of the American power elite set out in his most famous book, *The Power Elite* (1956), was a necessary first step in the unmasking of the deception that lay at the heart of the American way and, in turn, at the heart of modernity itself. Never before had there been so subtle an analysis of the social workings of power in the modern world. By contrast, Marx's implicit theory of power, while structurally brilliant, tripped over the extremes of his materialist code to such an extent that, with culture left out in the epiphenomenal wilderness, his politics floated skyward toward the ineffable contradiction. Power had no evident means to assert itself on the shop floor outside the abstract logic of capital accumulation. Twenty years after, Marx still did not quite get the lessons he taught in *The 18th Brumaire* on the political realities of 1848. It would be a good century after *Capital I* in 1867 before the recovery of Marx's early writings would begin to redress the abrasions left by Marx's all-too-crude top-down theory of power as a function of class effects.

Weber, a generation after Marx, hardly did better with his own, similarly vulgar definition of power as A's ability to dominate B. Like Marx, the mature social theory of power left by Weber was in the interstices—notably in the essay that was central to the collection Mills edited with Hans Gerth, *From Max Weber*: "Class, Status, and Party."[5] Though the essay itself is primarily one of Weber's most explicit accounts of his social theory of modern society as a series of differentiated spheres, its most salient contribution to the theory of power is the inclusion of status honor as, in effect, the *tertium quid* between raw economic power and political power. To the degree that Weber's theory of power was an implicit elaboration of the missing elements in Marx's class theory, then Mills's theory was an elaboration of the implicit elements in Weber's "Class, Status, and Party."

If, by today's standards, Mills's theory of power appears just as incomplete as, in further retrospect, do Marx's and Weber's, the insufficiency is a tribute to the author. *Power Elite* is the book that set the table for a full-blown theory of the ways modern power plays dirty tricks with culture. On the surface, Mills's idea of the higher circles of power in America would appear to be little more than a literary upgrading of Weber's "Class, Status, and Party":

> The elite who occupy the command posts may be seen as the possessors of power, wealth and celebrity: they may be seen as members of the upper stratum of a capitalistic society. They may also be defined in terms of psychological and moral criteria, as certain kinds of selected individuals. So defined, the elite, quite simply, are people of superior character and energy.[6]

With Mills there was always an edge, and here it cut toward culture as the joist that supports the powerful in their common interests: their moral criteria and character. The year before, 1955, Mills published an essay in *Dissent,* the very title of which might jolt the young who are more familiar with Michel Foucault's famous concept of *power/knowledge.* In "On Knowledge and Power," Mills wrote, "The problem of knowledge and power is, and always has been, the problem of the relations of men of knowledge with men of power."[7] This, of course, is a far cry from Foucault's reformulation of power theory in the early 1970s, but it is in a surprisingly more subtle theory of power (if not of culture) than that to be found in the book Foucault took as his point of departure, Herbert Marcuse's *One Dimensional Man* (1964), which became, even more than any writing of Mills, required reading of young radicals who came after 1962.[8]

What are the crucial differences between Mills and Marcuse that might have set Mills closer to Foucault? Very simply, though Mills's theory of power remained formally in the classic tradition of top-down theories (and thus in line with Marcuse's), it contained the elements that might have been (and probably were not) part of a new bottom-up theory of power. As raw as Mills's theory of culture was in comparison to Marcuse's ingenious doctrine of repressive desublimation in *One Dimensional Man,* in 1956 Mills already had a strong hunch that in the modern world power was never a thing in and of itself, but always an effect that works by its deceptive interminglings with culture, knowledge in particular. Exploitation and domination are raw power. But modern power, in times of peace and affluence like those of the 1950s, is a vastly more complex social thing. When at war, modern nations use force as terribly as did any other imperial order in history—worse, even. But in times of peace, when the logic of rational markets are at the fore, force is secondary to reason—to, that is, the efficient application of technical reason as if its calculations were at the essence of modern culture, which, of course, they were, and are.

Those of the generations younger by far than we who were young in 1962 may be surprised, as occasionally we are, that 1956—the year of *Power Elite*—was so thin as regards culture as today we think of it. Then, the most substantial theory of culture was to be found in Max Horkheimer and Theodor Adorno's *Dialectic of Enlightenment* (1947) which included the classic essay "The Culture Industry." But, as is well-known, even this seminal work, with its devastating assault on mass culture (including its failure to distinguish mass culture from popular culture), treated culture as still within the machinations of a dominant class, leaving culture as such to the honored traditions of high culture able to resist the social evil of capitalism and fascism. In 1956, in the United States where the German theorists were still largely unknown, the prevailing media of mass culture were radio and cinema. Television would not become a cultural force for a good decade. For Mills to have seen that the culture of the "men" of the higher circles was instrumental in bonding the power elite—thus in holding in place the structural filiations of their interlocking interests—was to see what would not become apparent to the naked eye for a good while to come. True, Mills's theory of power remained top-down, thus within the classical formulation. But also true, his theory moved light-years ahead of others in regarding the inner workings of the top-most elites as embedded in a necessary entanglement with their own culture (their "moral criteria") and with a vast array of institutional agents of their directors (which, in eerie anticipation of Louis Althusser's famous phrase, Mills called in a later essay "The Cultural Apparatus").[9]

One might say that all this probing for the special in a man of the 1950s is little more than an allegorical play on the filiation of ideas. In fact, while there is good evidence that Mills read the Europeans, there is no evidence that the French or even the Germans read Mills with any degree of avidity. But the idea is not to locate Mills at a node of intellectual progress so much as to account for his remarkable genius in imagining the history before him and the lessons that remain to be drawn from his example, as from his ideas.

Of all of Mills's writings, the one I find hardest to resist is the appendix to *The Sociological Imagination,* "On Intellectual Craftsmanship." This essay puts meat on the thin bones of the seminal concept of sociology as an imaginative exercise. In the title essay, Mills leaves imagination nicely formulated but poorly explored—too narrowly defined as an intellectual method, as if the issue-making structures were inaccessible for lack of knowledge. This, no doubt, was an artifact of the today-not-very-interesting subsequent attacks on Parsons ("Grand Theory") and sociological positivism ("Abstracted Empiricism"), which both did indeed propose that what the world needs now is sociological knowledge. But when Mills writes of craftsmanship, one begins to appreciate the method that allowed him, fixed as he was in a notably backward time, to step out of his times to see both what was wrong with his and what might be better in the ones to follow. He concludes with a list of advisories for those who imagine sociologically. Freely edited, the list was as follows:

1. Be a craftsman; avoid the fetishism of method and technique.

2. Avoid the mannerism of verbiage; urge upon yourself and others the simplicity of clear statement.
3. Make any transhistorical constructions you think your work requires; examine in detail the historical minutiae, but do not be a fanatic.
4. Do not study one small milieu after another; study the social structures in which milieux are organized.
5. Realize that your aim is a fully comparative understanding of the social structures; avoid the arbitrary specialization of prevailing academic departments.
6. Keep your eyes open to the varieties of individuality and to the modes of epochal change.
7. Know that you inherit and are carrying on the tradition of classic social analysis.
8. Do not allow public issues as they are officially formulated or troubles as they are privately felt, to determine the problems that you take up for study.[10]

It is one thing to give advice, another to follow it. Mills worked and lived by his own rules. The practical consequence was that he worked alone. He read others, and read them carefully. He wrote and spoke to others, with an evident sense of responsibility to their contributions and his place in the history he shared with them. But he worked and thought alone. This may well have aggravated the stress that broke his heart and killed him. It was certainly what he meant by the craft of the one who would imagine social things.

This quality of craft is what allowed him to see what was terribly wrong in the times he inherited—and he did not spare the labor metaphysic any more than the liberal nonsense of change arising on associations in civil society. And he certainly did not spare the stupidities of the main drift. Where others, such as the authors of the *Lonely Crowd* (1950), saw a tragic decline of the productive individual before the onslaught of consumer culture, Mills saw the late modern individual as tempted and trapped in the culture of postwar conformism but as also, and still, free to imagine, thus to make history. What saved Mills from the triumphalism of the liberal romance (the end of ideology and all that) was the irony of his method—both personal troubles and structured issues; both biography and large historical constructions; both critical and hopeful; both power and knowledge. Irony is the literary form that dwells on the both/and of the human situation, where tragedy sees the hero's fall as the end, and the comedic romance tidies up his life with a happy ending.

It has often been said, by Mills himself among others, that he did not quite grasp what was then so indelicately called the Negro problem in America. It is true, of course, that he did not, which is not the same thing as saying he would not have in due course. In 1962, the year of his death, few were the white academics of Mills's generation who understood anything at all about race in America. In the late 1950s and the early 1960s, the prevailing ignorances of the white academic elite, "men" [*sic*] roughly in midlife, were so much closer to my white-bread experiences than those of Tom Hayden and others at the founding of SDS. Had Mills lived to be at Port Huron, it seems likely that we would have learned something about race in America. But he would have also taught something about America in the world, something that would have likely taught my generation a lesson we did not begin to absorb until Vietnam came to the center of our concerns a good five or so years after he died.

The lesson even the best of whites on the Left were slow to learn was that the Negro problem in the South was not regional. Nor was it simply a national problem, as many finally began to understand after 1965. America's obsession with race—its most striking moral failure—was far more than an American problem. Race was, and is, global. If the modern world-system from 1500 on until perhaps 1989–1991 was a global system, it was global because it began in the simultaneous colonization of the lands of people of color, worldwide, and, most lucratively, in the capture of slaves for transport to the new colonies where they were pressed into the labor for the harvesting of spices and coffee, then cotton, which in turn were transshipped back to the U.S. Northeast and Western Europe for manufacture and production. Thus began modern capitalism in the world slave-trade triangle that linked Europe with the Americas by way of Africa, thus forming the Atlantic region that became the material and military base for the European Diaspora's global avarice. The towers of modern pride settled on race as the exploitative cement that laid the foundations for the profitable exploitation of human labor.

C. Wright Mills may not have understood these facts in just this way, but he understood them well before many of his followers. His naïveté in respect to the American race problem was, in effect, covered by this prescience with respect to the global situation. This is evident, if not perfectly evident, in the book that may have led to his death, *Listen, Yankee: The Revolution in Cuba* (1960). None of his books came closer to stirring public thinking and invective than this one, written after Mills visited Cuba shortly after Fidel Castro completed the revolution against the American capital interests that had colonized Cuba. So outraged was the liberal foreign policy establishment that it sent Adolf A. Berle, one of its slickest tongues, on the attack. Mills's first heart attack came on the eve of his scheduled national television debate with Berle, who relished the occasion to destroy Mills's brash argument that Cuba represented a ray of hope for change in the hemisphere and the world. No doubt had Mills debated Berle in December 1960, he would have been outclassed in the language and logic of the times. Kennedy had just been elected by the narrowest of margins in a contest with Richard Nixon, from whom the foreign policy differences were negligible. Four months later, on April 17, 1961, Kennedy ordered the Bay of Pigs invasion on the cold war wish that Castro, whatever he was politically, had to be a communist domino who could be toppled by the mere presence of the imperial guard on his shores. It would be a good long while before Cuba and the Caribbean, not to mention Africa and Southeast Asia, would begin to dawn on the American mind in terms that went beyond the narrow straights of American insular consciousness.

Yet, in a healthy retrospect, *Listen, Yankee* was a prophetic book. Not, it should be said, a good book. It reads today as slightly weird—still framed too much in the cold war rhetoric, still too optimistic as to the likelihood that Castro's political revolution would assure a social revolution, still too bound to the logic that any who opposed the American power elite were *ipso facto* on the side of progress. Yet, the single most striking literary feature of *Listen, Yankee* provides much more than a hint of where Mills would have gone had he survived 1962. First, and most contemptible to his opponents (who surely included the sociological methodologists), he wrote in the first person of a Cuban revolutionary. The conceit was that he could visit Cuba, meet with Fidel and Che, tour the country, and presume to write, but a few months after, in and for the voice of the Cuban people.

> So this is who we Cubans are:
> We're part of Latin America.
> We're fed up with Yankee corporations and governments.
> We've done something about it.
> Your corporations and your Government don't like it.
> We are not alone.[11]

Audacious, yes; but also telling, simple, and the truth of things to come. Remember his advice to the sociological imaginer: "Keep your eyes open to the varieties of individuality, and to the modes of epochal change." The sociological imagination as Mills worked it is not cautious, always willing to err, but also always open to the epochal changes the more cautious will miss. Even in *Listen, Yankee* Mills was working his power elite scheme. But he was willing to look beyond the American higher circles. Before Castro, Cuba suffered under the greedy fingers of the American power elite. Mills was quick to see that the revolution in Cuba was much more than a rebellion in an American off-shore colony. "We are not alone!" Mills understood that the Cuba of 1959 was part of a global movement, which meant that the United States was also bound by global necessities (an understanding that made little sense to the higher circles and the workers of their apparatus in 1960).

Mills may not have fully pictured the larger implications of the drift he was on at the time of his death. The imagination produces possibilities even the imaginer cannot fully see. Here, in the application of his method, is revealed the extent to which Mills himself went beyond sheer knowledge—mere facts—in the work of imagination. Too often, the facts of social things are interpreted in their retrospect—as structures that come down from the past. Structures do in fact come on us that way. But by the time they strike home, they are long dead. Still, they endure. The idea of the imagination is to dream without embarrassment—to study the facts of history and the feelings of personal life but to use knowledge to imagine a whole that is seldom visible to a naked eye that looks to the ground on the daily round.

Mills did not, it seems, have the least awareness of the now well-worn idea of the *imaginary*—a concept taken from the early writings of Jacques Lacan to describe the process whereby the whole is imagined to be more whole than ever it could be. Though, in 1969, Louis Althusser would famously put the concept to critical use in "Ideology and the Ideological State Apparatus," the imaginary can also serve good analytic purposes as it did in Benedict Anderson's *Imagined Communities: Reflections on the Origins and Spread of Nationalism* (1983).[12] Again, the point is not that Mills was an intellectual source of either. But there is something to be said for the qualities of his own intellectual craftsmanship that he was able to seize a word so close to another, the *imaginary*, that would take on conceptual importance of its own, thus to lend authority by association to Mills's concept, sociological imagination, that Mills made into a slogan that guided his thinking and that of others to come. For the sociological imagination, the imaginary is the structured world as a whole—as it can be reconstructed, never as it is as such, always as it seems to be becoming.

Cuba, in 1959, was in fact crucial to the imagination of those in North America alert to the possibilities of global change.

> As human beings, it is true, we Cubans have never had any close relations with you. But as peoples, each with its own govern-ment, now we are so far apart that there are Two Cubas—ours, and the one you picture to yourselves. And Two North Americas, too—yours, whatever it may be, and the one we think about in our country. Perhaps this would not matter so much were it not that we know our Cuba has become a new beginning in the Western Hemisphere, and maybe even in the world.[13]

How else is it possible to imagine the world as a whole, and to imagine it honestly, if one does not imagine the possibility that it is more than one? The modern world was one that could only be thought in twos that were hidden behind the myth of its oneness. The debate over binaries in modern thought cuts two ways at once—the critique of the primary We that diminishes the Other; and the reconsideration of the Other as a force in and of itself. Mills could think in twos while granting the differences as real and legitimate. He could assume the voice of the Other in Cuba, perhaps, because he got the picture; he saw the others for what they were and for how they imagined the world about them.

"The colonial world is a world cut in two."[14] This was Frantz Fanon in 1961 in *Wretched of the Earth*. Fanon was for the most part unknown in America in the year Mills died. Within a few years, his book would stand with Marcuse's *One Dimensional Man* as a field guide for young revolutionaries who, like me, never imagined such wild birds could fly. It would be the revolutionary thinkers of Africa and Martinique, not of Cuba, who would put detail on the imaginary of the Other invisible to the global power elite. Still, Mills was moving in a direction that would suggest he understood that, in the deeper recesses of global structures, the two imaginaries were moving decisively against each other. Castro's revolutionary in 1959 was part of the global movement Mills seemed to have understood without fully being able to say why and how.

Fanon lay dying of cancer in December 1961, just months before Mills would drop dead. By 1962, the white student leaders at Michigan were setting Mills's words to music even we dull ones could march to. As Fanon lay dying, black students in Greensboro, North Carolina, were crystallizing national attention on the by-then already-well-developing southern movement against racial structures. Neither blacks nor whites of those days would fully see the global picture until after 1966, which was the year we put the ironic words into Muhammad Ali's mouth: "No Viet Cong ever called me Nigger." Race is a global thing. American racism is part and parcel of its global attitude. Ali, without having heard of Fanon, got the picture. "The colonial world is a world divided in two." If it is, then the allegiances of the colonized are with their brothers and sisters wherever they are. It was then, in the conjuncture of decolonizing forces already well under way in 1962, that the imagined community of the global nation-state was called into question in the open—called out, that is, for all to see. Muhammad Ali was indeed a big mouth, but not in the sense his detractors meant. He had the moral might to broadcast his musings around the globe. As they traveled, they gathered. up the attention of those who, like him, were unable to read Fanon or Mills.

C. Wright Mills belonged to another time. But he was not rooted in those times. It makes little sense today to engage in the *What if he had survived 1962?* From a rude historical point of view, he had to die when he did. In either case, he died before the epochal changes he sensed were coming came into the open, and this may be why a book like *Radical Nomad* is so important today to those of us who did not die in our youth. There are, of course, countless books on the history of the 1950s, but there are few quite so to the point that requires our attentions in the early years of the 2000s. We live in a very different time, but we live in a time different because of the changes Mills had begun to see and explore. To read this sparkling account of Mills's thinking by a man, Hayden, who has since been a maker of the history that came after is to read of the generative process one must go through if one is to imagine the imaginary of any time.

Perhaps the single most obdurate barrier to the sociological imagination is the natural human reluctance to remember bad dreams. It is all the more pleasant to embrace the good times. The 1950s in which Mills worked were such a time—good times down at the old frat house drinking beer and chasing girls as a way out and away from the bad dreams all over that temporal place. Friends were killed. Parents blackballed. Racial jokes made (and ignored). Alleged traitors vilified. Wars started. Yet, the great white unwashed generally fooled around. Our parents tried to keep us from grinding hips with Elvis. They feared that he might really be as his music sounded—if not a commie, at least a Negro. And so we who were slow to rise to the bad dreams of those good times stood by for a few years more as those inspired by Mills began to make the history we eventually entered, there to remain for the rest of our days now ending. Dylan was our Elvis. We made love, to be sure, but we also made war on the silliness of our youth, which was, of course, the world we as kids looked out upon in discomfort.

It is far more than historical curiosity that recommends *Radical Nomad* in these times of our pending endings. Mills worked through a mind-numbing time that was far from good. Others knew something was wrong, but, like Riesman, they could only picture it as the tragic fall of the good modern, American way of discipline and productivity. Most were trapped in a nostalgia for a what-was, which in fact never had been. Mills went to the heart of the matter. Power was held by the higher circles, true. But power, Mills realized, was also in the hands of those subjected to the powerful elites, if only they would imagine a better world—which was decidedly not a fun one, not even a good one. Mills's better world was the world as it was; a world one had to live in, as long as one could, weak of heart and all, telling the bad news of the sociological imagination until, at long last, someone had the decency to say, "Enough!"

Notes

1. C. Wright Mills, *Letters and Autobiographical Writings,* ed. Kathryn Mills with Pamela Mills (Berkeley: University of California Press, 2000), 321.

2. Wallerstein, "Time and Duration: The Unexcluded Middle, or Reflections on Braudel and Prigogine," in *The Uncertainties of Knowledge* (Philadelphia: Temple University Press, 2004), 34–58.

3. The text was published as "What We Want," in *Dissent* (Fall 1966). The reference to Waveland is a play on time. The 1964 Waveland staff meeting of SNCC was the beginning of the divide within and between black and white student movements. Like Port Huron, SNCC was a youth movement directed at the failure of old order to distinguish black politics from white rhetoric.

4. Charles Lemert, *Muhammad Ali: Trickster in the Culture of Irony* (Oxford: Polity, 2003), 86–119.

5. Hans Gerth and C. Wright Mills, *From Max Weber* (New York: Oxford University Press, 1946), 180–94.

6. *The Power Elite* (New York: Oxford University Press, 1965), 13.

7. "On Knowledge and Power" in *Power, Politics, and People: The Collected Essays of C. Wright Mills,* ed. Irving Louis Horowitz (New York: Ballantine Books, 1963), 606.

8. The allusion to Foucault is to the repressive hypothesis (for which, it seems, Marcuse was the model), the criticism in his first full statement of his bottom-up theory of power, *History of Sexuality, I* (New York: Vintage Books, 1978); compare Marcuse, *One Dimensional Man* (Boston: Beacon, 1964).

9. Ibid., 405–22.

10. *The Sociological Imagination* (New York: Oxford University Press, 1959), 224–26.

11. *Listen, Yankee: The Revolution in Cuba* (New York: Ballantine Books, 1960), 28–29.

12. Anderson, *Imagined Communities: Reflections on the Origins and Spread of Nationalism* (New York: Verso, 1983). Althusser's "Ideology and the Ideological State Apparatus" appears in *Lenin & Philosophy and Other Essays* (New York: Monthly Review Press, 1971).

13. *Listen, Yankee: The Revolution in Cuba* (New York: Ballantine Books, 1960).

14. Frantz Fanon, *Wretched of the Earth* (New York: Grove, 1963), 38.

Introduction

Missing Mills

Tom Hayden

IT WAS A WARM MARCH MORNING IN ATLANTA, AND I WAS sitting in bed drinking coffee. I finally had finished the draft of the manifesto of Students for a Democratic Society (SDS), which became known as the Port Huron Statement. The document was strongly influenced by C. Wright Mills's independent radicalism, especially his "Letter to the New Left" in which he declared that "the Age of Complacency is ending." The founding convention of SDS in Port Huron, Michigan, was three months away. The civil rights and student movements were exploding "out of apathy"—another phrase of Mills's. Epic change, we were certain, was blowing in the wind.

Then my pleasant morning was shattered: A *New York Times* headline in front of me reported that "C. Wright Mills, a Sociologist," was dead of a heart attack at age forty-five. I experienced chest pain and can still relive the depression that began that moment.

It was an omen of things to come. In the great movement that was beginning, euphoria and idealism would be balanced by death, and death again, by bullets but also by burnout and betrayal. Mills, it seemed, had been exhausted by a long, lonely struggle against the system he named "the power elite." Recovering from a massive 1960 heart attack, he wrote, "What we do not now know as yet is how much intellectual and moral tension I can stand.... What bothers me is whether the damned heart will stand up to what ... must be done."[1]

None of us in SDS knew him, though many were followers. After Albert Camus and Bob Dylan, Mills ranked as the most pervasive influence on the first generation of SDS. He was the mentor, perhaps the father figure, I needed at the time. Even today I think of him as a sort of absent parent.

SDS members grew up either in the mass society Mills described in *White Collar* or within the Old Left he examined in *The Marxists.* More than any other thinker, he placed our lives in a meaningful context. I was the son of a divorced corporate accountant and school librarian in one of Detroit's first suburbs. My parents were those members of the new middle class Mills perfectly described as lacking any ability to connect the problems of their personal lives with larger structural causes. They were apolitical, apathetic, tending to blame themselves for any shortcomings. Mills diagnosed the serious need to somehow turn their personal troubles into political issues.

Other SDS founders, such as Dick and Mickey Flacks or Steve Max, had been raised in the culture of the Old Left, which was battered by McCarthyism, demoralized by Stalinism, and marginalized by the expansion of the suburban middle class. They, too, needed the fresh ideological beginning that Mills offered.

The growth of this fifties middle class discredited what Mills called the "labor metaphysic" of the Old Left, the dogmatic belief in one big working class. Instead, he said, American society had become a mass society whose class lines were blurred.

Out of this white-collar middle class burst the New Left, living proof that the mass society had not deadened the will to protest. The triggering revolt was the black student movement in the South, a phenomenon Mills paid little attention to, which catalyzed the larger middle class "youth revolt" of the era. In the background was a global revolutionary upheaval starting with African liberation movements, the Cuban Revolution, and, finally, the Vietnamese resistance, all of which challenged the dangerous nuclear premises of the bipolar cold war that Mills criticized in *The Causes of World War Three.*

With his "Letter to the New Left" and "Listen Yankee," Mills explained how the youth rebellions and anticolonial struggles were two different responses to a single, suffocating power elite devoted to obsessive anticommunism. In these later years, he both described and encouraged the revival of a "democratic public" in place of the mass society, or "democracy without publics," of the fifties. He himself was not a joiner; his old friend Saul Landau remembers Mills as an "astute observer and a man who didn't easily tolerate hypocrites, but I never saw him go to a demo or refer to having gone to one."[2] He was a radical nomad.[3] But, oh, he had a force.

The 1960 heart attack felled Mills as he prepared for a nationally televised debate over Cuba and Latin America with Adolph A. Berle, a symbol of the sort of intellectuals whom Mills accused of celebrating the status quo. Mills would live two more years, but there was little doubt that he was ground to death by a lack of support in his one-man crusade. The "furor" over Mills's pamphlet on Cuba, according to Dan Wakefield, "led to mounting pressures that clearly contributed to Mills's early death."[4] Berle himself expressed a shocking smugness over Mills's collapse, calling him a "ranting propagandist" and even claiming that "he got a heart attack—partly I think because he was frightened—and had reason to be."[5] A sympathetic biographer of Mills, Irving Louis Horowitz, in writing of Mills's death, also made a chastising reference, comparing Mills to a Joseph Conrad figure, Nostromo: "Here was a man that seemed as though he would have preferred to die rather than deface the perfect form of his egoism. Such a man was safe."[6]

I began to write a thesis on Mills for graduate school in Ann Arbor in 1963, identifying with him as a "radical nomad." Having fully absorbed his thinking and style, I then left graduate school in summer 1964, to see whether I could carry his lessons into practice, and whether practice might produce further evidence of its own. My thesis remained on my shelf until Dean Birkenkamp of Paradigm Publishers kindly offered to place it in the public domain. I am honored that Dick Flacks and Stanley Aronowitz, two of my intellectual mentors at the time, have added their perspectives to this memorializing of Mills along with respected sociologist, Charles Lemert.

Reading the manuscript today, I am struck first by how things have changed from the days of messy duplicating machines to computers. My rhetoric then was that of a graduate student full of himself. My thesis, like the work of Mills, was devoid of any reference to women, whose liberation movement would surface just after the manuscript was completed. Nor to gays, lesbians, and environmentalists, the activists just beyond the limits of my experience.

That Mills, at age forty-five, missed the social and public significance of women, was typical of male thinkers and activists of the time. Women were assumed to be extensions of men, often invisible, without autonomous identities. For example, while I was immersed in writing about Mills, I was hardly aware that my marriage was falling apart. Thinking only of myself, I had moved with my wife, Sandra "Casey" Cason, to graduate school at the University of Michigan. A central and charismatic leader of the southern student civil rights movement, Casey took an unfulfilling job as a secretary in Ann Arbor to support us and promptly began to wilt as I plunged into my intellectual challenges. Mills was no help as a role model here. Casey went on, with Mary King, to draft the first "notes on women's liberation" in response to the treatment of women in the early movement.

I do not blame Mills for my chauvinism, but if he had written a book describing the elite as *male* or as a *patriarchy* as powerful as the capitalists and militarists, I might have been more conscious. As a sociologist, too, Mills might have discerned the invisible disparities and contradictions faced by working women instead of describing the mass society of the fifties as hopelessly frozen and monolithic. He did not predict the women's movement as he did the New Left and anticolonial struggles. Simone de Beauvoir alone is mentioned in a 1959 Mills letter and in "Radical Nomad" as well.[7] In fairness, Betty Friedan's *The Feminine Mystique,* about the invisible suffering of women in mass society, was not published until the year of Mills's death.

The same might be said of his attitudes toward race. "I have never been interested in what is called 'the Negro problem,'" he wrote in a letter. "The truth is, I've never looked into it as a researcher. I have a feeling that if I did it would turn out to be a 'white problem' and I've got enough of those on my hands just now.... The US of A is a white tyranny. It will remain so until there is no distinction whatsoever drawn in marriages between the races."[8] This was a privatized view of race relations at a time when thousands of young black (and white) people were going to jail in the South to challenge elite rule. His "Letter to the New Left" did credit them as an agency of change conducting "direct non-violent action, and it seems to be working, here and there. Now we must learn from their practice and work out with them new forms of action."[9] But he went no further. While he traveled to Cuba and dramatically reported its revolution, he never visited the South during the 1955 Montgomery bus boycott or the 1960s sit-ins.

Mills felt much closer to the Mexicans, learning from his Spanish-speaking mother that "Mexicans have always formed her ideal images of the Human Being." He told his mother that "the Cubans are my Mexicans."[10]

This empathy with Mexicans is typical of Irish American Catholics, a connection that Mills never seemed to recognize. The almost total detachment from his Irish heritage limited his understanding of the price the white-collar middle classes paid by assimilation. *The mass society, after all, was the assimilated society,* producing an anxiety that had no name for most striving white ethnics (and to a lesser extent, people of color). Mills, whose Irish Catholic family was driven out of Ireland during the Famine times (a background I shared with him), never discussed being Irish except in a 1943 letter to his colleague Hans Gerth. I quote from the letter extensively, highlighting the anguished portions that appear as symptoms of the inability to assimilate into the dominant WASP culture of the time:

> Last Friday I was working at the office at night on motives chapter and sort of collapsed emotionally and "spiritually." For about two hours, I realized later, I just sat and stared at the row of books, with the light on in the office and rest of the building all dark. It was the oddest feeling and I can't explain it. Like a trance, only all the time I was thinking about war and the *hopelessness of things*. It was as if you were thinking—yes, you have to use that word—with a *sequence of moods*. The polarity probably was between *helplessness* and *aggressiveness* and both were, I think, rather relished! Also for the first time, except in what was, explicitly at least, in fun, I had a self-image of being very *Irish*. ... *I do not know why because I do not know anything about "the Irish"* and I have never, to my knowledge, been stamped as Irish by anyone particularly. I think maybe it is all because of the *inarticulate feelings of indignation* that come up when I confront politics in any serious way and because I cannot locate and denounce ... such enemies as are available....
>
> Living in an atmosphere soaked in lies, the man who thinks, at least, that he knows some of the truth but would lose his job were he to tell it out and is not man enough to do it anyway ... if such a man has built such a life around finding out the truth and being aggressive with it, then *he suffers*. I wrote a lot more, and even began a short story [as follows]:
>
> What happened was that *the self-distance and the use of self for objective work* which was usual with him had collapsed. It collapsed and *he saw another self for a while*. And what he saw was a political man. He had not known before that the well of indignation which had become his basic political feeling was masking such strong political urges.

These are masked *Irish* feelings, not "Texas outsider" feelings as some have argued. Mills died one year before the assassination of President John Kennedy, who in 1960 symbolized the story of successful assimilation—just before his death and the unfolding of other Kennedy family tragedies that suggested an Irish fate rather than the immigrants' triumph. Mills never looked at suppressed ethnic worries beneath the white collar, where he might have discovered how the mass society served to perpetuate status-based shame, inferiority, and feelings of helplessness. The strain of smothering such unconscious feelings can kill a man, or so I believe today. Instead, Mills accepted the prevalent view of the triumphal "melting pot" that became for him the mass society, just at the moment when a *reverse assimilation* was beginning in all spheres of American culture. That is one reason that Mills became relatively forgotten amid the later emphasis on multi-culturalism. Perhaps now a return to his analytic framework, including the dimensions of racial, ethnic, and gender identity, might help us achieve an integrated Big Picture once again.

Across the decades I still feel his loss. In retrospect, it should be said that he established in his life and work, for myself and many others, the definition of what it means to be an "intellectual," one who attempts to clarify where we fit in the larger scheme of things, and what it means to be an "agent of social change," one who participates in making history from below.

This is a time of eerie similarities with the fifties. The cold war framework has been replaced by that of a permanent War on Terrorism, and McCarthyism by the Patriot Act. On the other hand, new social movements, especially in the global South, threaten the glib assumptions of an omnipotent market economy and military hegemony. And where are the intellectuals? As in Mills's time, too many are occupied with celebrations of the triumph of capitalism over communism in the cold war and the rise of a de facto American Empire. Once again they claim that there are no systemic alternatives to the status quo, that history has ended. Still others limit themselves to specialized research that has little public benefit.

Yet there is a rising global hunger for systemic explanations of our plight. Audiences as large as twenty-five thousand listen eagerly to Noam Chomsky, Naomi Klein, and Arundahti Roy at world social forums in Brazil or India. The right questions are being asked again. Who is collecting, sorting, and analyzing the shadowy new elites of power? Has Mills's concept of the power elite now been globalized in agencies such as the World Trade Organization (WTO), and how can transnational structures be exposed and confronted by transnational movements? Are we oscillating between empire and a multipolar world, or are social movements creating space for a more participatory world of multicultural democracy?

I for one wish Mills could be present for the discussion. In his absence, I hope that his legacy of power structure research will be revived and applied to globalization. And I hope that his infectious populist enthusiasm is communicated and carried on among those today who resist empire in new social movements, such as the Seattle shutdown of the WTO in 1999, the numerous other "Seattles" of recent years, and the unprecedented global movement against the Iraq war. These quite spontaneous movements once again surprise the elites and threaten their hegemony. They contain a clear continuity from the day that Mills's heart gave out. The causes of World War III have not been prevented so much as expanded. The mass societies today must choose between entertainment and engagement. The political parties must wake up or be abandoned. The media must begin to notice that the people are restless for independent news.

The Left is dead again; the Left is born again. As Mills said shortly before he died, we must study these new movements as "real live agencies of social change." And, I would add, join them. All movements begin at the margins, when the surface is peaceful and the pundits are sleeping. But they erupt unpredictably, march to the mainstream eventually, and become majorities in their time, clashing with the Machiavellian power elites, achieving reforms, finally fading into our blurred and brainwashed memories, exhausted, until the radical nomads find renewed resonance in the next generation.

Notes

1. C. Wright Mills, *Letters and Autobiographical Writings,* ed. Kathryn Mills with Pamela Mills (Berkeley: University of California Press, 2000), 324.

2. Personal correspondence, 2005.

3. "I am a politician without a party," he wrote, "a writer without any of the cultural background" [of a born writer], and "a man who feels most truly alive only when working"; in Mills, *Letters,* 303.

4. Mills, *Letters,* 5.

5. Cited in Irving Louis Horowitz, *C. Wright Mills: An American Utopian* (New York: Free Press, 1983), 301.

6. Horowitz, *C. Wright Mills,* 302.

7. Mills called de Beauvior "an admirable woman … whom you ought read, especially if you are a woman or know any women," in a letter to Tovarich in 1959. See Mills, *Letters,* 276.

8. Mills, *Letters,* 314.

9. Mills, *Letters,* 307.

10. Mills, *Letters,* 313–15.

Postrevolutionary Society?

C. Wright Mills's creative lifetime spanned a fantastic period in American and world history. Throughout the 1940s and 1950s social theorists have struggled to make sense of this history and have developed quite polar interpretations of the new social systems in the advanced industrial societies.

Some theories picture a new Leviathan. Whether described as a collectivist bureaucracy, a technological totalitarianism, a mass society, or a managerial authoritarianism, its main consequence is the crushing of individual creativity and freedom. Other theories propose that men have progressed to a new place of hope, whether described as the welfare state, enterprise democracy, or the postindustrial society.

What both these streams of interpretation share, however, is the agreement that revolutionary social change, in the sense of organized popular movements transferring political power from an alien set of leaders to themselves, is no longer likely in industrial countries. Different theorists cite various sources of this end-of-revolution. The pessimists stress totalitarianism, manipulation, the "massification" of Western men, the availability of material benefits to distressed groups, and the propaganda power inherent in the new systems of mass communication. The more optimistic observers, in their turn, tend to list abundance, the enfranchisement of all groups in the political state, and the managed stabilization of economic development. Whatever the cause, however, the dominant agreement has been that a new *postrevolutionary epoch* is being achieved in the Western countries. It is as if a long bridge was crossed, then burned, from the crisis situation of the 1930s to the stability of the postwar period.

C. Wright Mills was a revolutionary, but without a movement, without intellectual company, without an ideology for revolution. None of the Enlightenment philosophies of reason and freedom, including Marxism most specifically, could satisfactorily explain, for Mills, the agencies and the means of constructing a new society. The working class of Western societies seemingly had accepted the welfare-capitalist system; the intellectuals had been conscripted into nationalist loyalty; the common people had been transformed into the personally helpless condition characteristic of mass society.

Mills plunged ahead in an examination of the society that apparently had obviated the base of social revolution and thus created his isolation. In succession, he studied organized labor; an ethnic minority; the new middle classes of dependent employees; the hierarchies of political, economic, and military power; the celebrities; the intellectuals; the liberal and radical movements. That he could visualize and integrate the new currents—the emergence of the three bureaucratic elites out of World War II, the stabilizing of Western capitalist economies, the arch-fascination of men with military posturing and the cold war, the development of widespread political indifference in the middle and lower classes, the merging of liberalism into the political center, the decline of the American left—made him the most thoroughgoing observer of the American way of life in his times. That he could see *through* these forms—through the hypocrisy, fraud, obfuscation, privilege, irrationality, and totalitarianism—made him the impassioned voice of protest of his time. His work was a symphony of science and sensibility, insight and eloquence, and always contained the rough beauty of the unfinished. He was a lonely and prophetic workman, a radical nomad. He inspired hundreds of intellectuals to become "cultural workers" as well, blending their values and their skills in the birth of a new social theory to clarify modern conditions. He inspired thousands more to end their troubled peace with society and begin a troubled critique. He gave hope to thousands in other lands that this land might one day achieve its full democratic possibilities. Even his angriest critics—those of the traditional Left and the liberal celebrants of the going show—displayed a magnetized attachment to his career and carried on a continuous debate about his work and his future.

This book is an intellectual biography of a man whose ideas were among the most serious of the last generation. The development of his work can be divided into four periods:

- Apprehension and Maturation, 1939–1949
- Pessimism Formulated: The Analysis of the Power Elite and the Mass Society, 1950–1956
- Radical Polemics: Analyzing the Default, 1956–1960
- Tentative Hopes: The New Left, 1960–1962

Apprehension and Maturation, 1939–1949

In this period, Mills completed a number of essays on sociology, especially the sociology of knowledge; he initiated his research on the business and political elites; and he published, with Hans Gerth, translations of Max Weber, *From Max Weber: Essays in Sociology* (1946); and a book on the labor movement, *The New Men of Power* (1948). During this period his stance was independent, but definitely within the radical tradition of opposing a corporate-capitalist political economy with a hope for a democratic political movement with the working class at its center. The seeds of his later conceptions, especially of enlarging military power, were present in this period in awkward form.

Pessimism Formulated: The Analysis of the Power Elite and the Mass Society, 1950–1956

In these years, Mills's sociological research and analysis culminated, first in his study of the middle classes, *White Collar* (1950); then in his book with Hans Gerth on social theory, *Character and Social Structure* (1953); and finally in the opus *The Power Elite* (1956). The period actually began with *The Puerto Rican Journey* (1950), done with Rose Goldsen and Clarence Senior, a book that first began to formulate the pessimism that destroyed Mills's hope in the working class. In the later books this theme was developed elaborately: At the bottom of society a "mass" was replacing classes and publics, while at the top a power elite was expropriating the means not only of production but also of communications, politics, and war—the conditions of popular sovereignty. This was his richest period of research on American society, and the quality of Mills's writing added a dramatic tone that shaped his characterization of the new society. But if his vision was burning, it was also grieved. To the extent the power elite and the mass society were actual facts rather than approaching tendencies, there was no chance for protest or revolt. Yet Mills could not let the chance disappear.

Radical Polemics: Analyzing the Default, 1956–1960

This period involved Mills more than ever in the search for a source of radical power, an agency of social change. His isolation—indeed, the isolation of all American radicals—was so complete that his writing turned into bitter inquiries into the default of the liberal and radical movements, and especially into the default of the intellectuals in their role as guardians of reason and freedom. He entered the political arena with his tracts on *The Causes of World War Three (1958)* and on Cuba, *Listen, Yankee* (1960). He fought against the asocial drift of academia by reasserting the classic sociological tradition in *The Sociological Imagination* (1959) and

Images of Man (1960). He continued to exist in profound loneliness on the American scene, though his own works were increasingly a matter of public attention and, usually, attack.

Tentative Hopes: The New Left, 1960–1962

The analysis of the default brought Mills to a more intense consideration of the problem of agencies of change, a consideration that took him to the international scene and, finally, to the discovery that young intellectuals, especially in the new nations, were key members of revolutionary movements. In the "overdeveloped" societies, too, he found, the young intellectuals were breaking out of apathy into new forms of analysis and action. Despite his enthusiasm for these "new beginnings," he began to see the crisis of the times as one of political philosophy—there was no available and adequate explanation of how humanist goals could be realized in an antihuman age. As Mills was still assuming a long-term stabilization of Western capitalism, but beginning to wonder with excitement about the possibilities for change in the new countries and perhaps even in the West, this was a time of fertile expansion and transition in Mills's career.

Mills died on March 21, 1962. He was only forty-five years old. The cause of death was the coronary condition that he had developed and aggravated throughout the 1950s.

I remember my whole body hardening when I came upon the obituary in the *New York Times*. It was as though his own powerful physical system, thrown unrelentingly into the grinding process of his mission, broke down in desperation and futility. For me it symbolized the shattering isolation and collapse of American radicalism against a fundamentally overpowering system.

In the subsequent months I began to reread Mills, trying to formulate the questions so mysteriously posed by his death. This, then, is a frankly partisan work, which begins and ends with an enormous empathy for the intellectual and political struggle of

C. Wright Mills. It is rooted in a belief, one that Mills would have cheered, in participatory democracy where men together make the decisions that order and direct their lives, where abundance is used the world over for the common good, and love comes to be more universally felt. If these ends cannot be secured in a lifetime, some of them certainly can and must be, and it is the beauty of hope for the rest that fires this work.

Despite its central intent, however, this book might even be of interest in circles where partisanship is considered bigotry and a form of intellectual failing. This is not a manifesto but an agonized inquiry into the problems of power, freedom, and change in a profoundly unusual period: one of war, cold war, radical technological change, and new power alignments. There is nothing in partisanship that ruins analysis; we all quest in different ways, and since our quests make or contribute to history, they should be openly considered and integrated in our analysis of current history. Intellectuals long sought that freedom from society that we know as "objectivity." This book assumes, however, that freedom begins with the admission that one's actions count and that therefore one is accountable for knowing the myriad ways in which his action contributes to his writing and to the circumstances about which he writes. In this work, there will be no division of "fact" from "value"; instead, it hopes to communicate what one man sees, how and why he sees it, and what he makes of it.

The questions posed, at least symbolically, in the passing of Mills are, What kind of society so effectively destroyed radical protest? Is the basis of protest and revolution really dead in America?

Chapter 1

Postwar Beginnings

An Independent Left Perspective

*T*HE *NEW MEN OF POWER* (1948) WAS BOTH A STUDY OF American labor leaders and a major analysis of the structure of American society and its future. It was perhaps the closest Mills came in the 1940s or 1950s to a political statement in general sympathy with an orthodox left-wing view of social change. Scrutinized carefully, it reveals, not simply some early gropings toward the later theory of the power elite, but it reflects the society of the middle and late 1940s, in which uncertainty about political directions existed to considerable degree, as opposed to the society of the 1950s, which, to Mills, represented an overpowering stability.

As Mills worked on *The New Men of Power,* World War II was ending. To many Americans this was only a partial relief, since it portended the resumption of the older economic difficulties and social struggles of the 1930s that had been suspended during the war. The core of these troubles was the apparent inability of the American economy to achieve full employment and security for the working class and realize its potential of abundance for all. When the war began, depression still blighted the country; for example, in 1939, 9.5 million were out of work, or 17.2 percent of the labor force. As Mills would later write in *The Sociological*

Imagination, the 1930s were a "political age," in which structural issues were evident and commonly felt. The struggle to organize the industrial working class; the widespread involvement of the intellectuals in public debate and action; the political furies surrounding and permeating the New Deal administration; the new historical "alternatives" of Nazi Germany and Socialist Russia that America seemed forced to choose between—there were these and many other ingredients of social conflict over the direction of American society. Then came the war, and with it the decline of nearly all forms of "left versus right" conflict. Indeed, this course was even advocated. Bruce Catton's history of the period describes as the view of many industrial leaders: "The war could not be won unless there was national unity, and there couldn't be national unity unless the nation bought off its critics by desisting from the actions of which the critics complained. It made a lovely game, and the tragedy was that the administration wasn't able to stand up against it." Catton quoted a symbolic speech by one industrial leader who argued, "America is losing the war for one fundamental reason and only one: our government—meaning primarily the president of the United States—still stubbornly persists in the attempt simultaneously to fight a foreign war and wage an internal economic revolution—and wars are not, never were and never can be won that way." This may have been a rather extreme formulation; there is evidence, for example, that some major business leaders feared that too much profit pyramiding would backlash against industry after the war. Biographer Arnold Rogow writes that James Forrestal, president of Dillon, Read in 1939 and later secretary of defense, prescribed a relatively "cautious" line by businessmen in order to maintain their overall interests.

The expanding war economy fully employed all who were able to work. Government-business-labor agreements curbed the right to strike. Former opponents became temporary allies. An uneasiness prevailed, however, about the viability of America in peacetime. Continued political conflict seemed inevitable, and, to Mills and others, it held out at least the possibility of radical change through working-class action.

However, Mills could see another possibility, to him a more likely one. This was the entrenchment of a bureaucratic "liberal" state, dominated by the giant corporations, defended and subtly shaped by the new military hierarchy, accepted by the new labor leaders, and largely invisible to the scattered and confused publics. He suspected that "a tacit sort of plan to stabilize the political economy of the US is back of many current demands of the spokesmen of the three powerful bureaucracies in the US political economy." The biggest strategists of the stabilization were the "sophisticated conservatives"—an elite that "leaves the noise" to the less powerful and more reactionary right-wingers; which "works in and among other elite groups, primarily the high military, the chieftains of large corporations, and certain politicians"; which holds that "unions are a stabilizing force and should be encouraged as a counter-force against radical movements." Mills envisioned the amalgamation of the union bureaucracy with the corporation. He believed this already was happening in the workplace, where, for example, several major unions were entering agreements to prevent "unauthorized" strikes by the rank and file, in exchange for jurisdictional stability and corporate recognition of union legitimacy. Especially with the American Federation of Labor (AFL) still pushing hard to replace the new Congress of Industrial Organizations (CIO) where it had been established, the steel, auto, and other industrial unions were willing to sign "mutual responsibility clauses" by which employers or employees who fomented the "unauthorized stoppages of work" were financially liable and subject to discharge.

Agreements for stability on an industry-wide basis were developing also. For instance, in garment and other industries where a single union dealt with a large number of small businessmen, the union was the most stable element in the entire industry and took the primary role as the stabilizing agent. In such agreements, the union accepted the premise of free enterprise and demanded efficiency in return. Cooperation between unions and management on this basis, according to capitalist theory, makes business and union more cost-conscious and therefore increases the earnings of the workers, managers, and others. In order to prevent instability due to competition among free enterprisers, wage- and price-setting techniques for an entire industry are then sought: "on the industry level, true cooperation rather than compromise is possible: all the corporations forming the industry, along with the industry-wide union, can pass on to the consumers [in the end, mostly to workers in other industries] the higher costs involved and thus maintain high profits and high wages." For instance, the chairman of the Steelworkers Organizing Committee declared in the 1930s that if the steel corporations "cannot put their house in order, it is the avowed purpose of the organized steel workers in this nation to promote a constructive legislative program that will adequately protect the interests of the industry and its workers." Fearing that cutthroat competition would force wages to spiral downward and upset union stability, the steelworkers supported delays of federal investigations into the steel monopoly in 1938.

For Mills, the trend to stabilization at the plant and industry levels pointed logically in the direction of business-labor cooperation in stabilizing the national political economy itself, with the participation of the state. In this "liberal state," seeking domestic stability and international security, there would be a unity of aim between government and the corporations, and the steady attrition of the union movement. Mills correctly saw in the New Deal the beginning of the trend. It was "an attempt to subsidize the defaults of the capitalist system," consisting in the effort to "rationalize business and labor as systems of power in order to permit a continued flow of profits, investment and employment." He saw in the National Industrial Recovery Act (NIRA) the birth of a corporate state where within each industrial combine the employers and employees are unified and sovereignty is given to monopoly unions and trade associations in their narrow spheres, and to trade and labor associations in their common spheres of action.

NIRA was terminated after two years by a 1935 Supreme Court decision, but not, according to Mills, because of solid national consensus against its conceptual basis. It died because of the insufficient power of enforcement delegated to FDR; the weakened but continued opposition of small businessmen to monopoly capital; the ideological rifts in the still-developing union movement; and temporary improvements in the economy that relieved some of the pressure toward the corporate-state solution. The 1935 National Labor Relations Act (the Wagner Act), although it contained the democratic principle of rank-and-file selection of union representatives, "came into being under the spell, as it were, of the corporate state idea behind the NIRA and the experience of the boards operating under the NIRA. In the sequence of political fact, the Wagner Act was adopted to replace the NIRA when it ended." It was meant to equalize bargaining power between employee and employer and therefore prevent economic depressions caused by competitive wage rates and working conditions. Union power here became dependent on other forces besides its strength in direct relation to the employer—chief among these were the majority will of the employees and the operation of the sanctioning governmental framework.

The Taft-Hartley amendment to the Wagner Act, passed in 1947 just prior to the publication of *The New Men of Power,* pointed further in the direction of a business attempt, with the support of government, at regulation and compulsory arbitration of disputes. Increasingly, in Mills's view, the state would become the regulator of the national labor force. Here Mills was upholding a basic Marxian perspective: "Contrary to the liberal theory of the state, the government is not a neutral umpire using its impartial wisdom to effect a fair balance; it is increasingly a political instrument of employers, or at least a new amalgamation of business and governmental power." It would be several years before he decided it was the latter. In the meantime, he criticized the labor leaders for facilitating this trend by their reliance on government, instead of the worker, for their solutions; and for their refusal to think of themselves as a "potential majority movement with which to re-organize modern society." The small business antagonism to unions furthered the "Main Drift," too, he thought, by causing such national turmoil that "the public" comes to demand that the state intervene, that somebody do something: "In Italy, Germany, Austria, and Spain somebody did something." Mills came close to but never specifically predicted the "guidelines" policies of the 1960s, in which all the power of the federal government is brought to bear, though not quite institutionalized, in order to settle bargaining disputes without changing the constant ratio of wages, profits, and production levels.

This view of the "Main Drift" was prelude to *White Collar* and, finally, to Mills's most thorough theoretical statement, *The Power Elite.* What did not appear after 1948 was Mills's view of the means of social change, or arresting the Main Drift, which appeared in *The New Men of Power.* He expressed in 1948 a radical program with greater unity of vision and strategy than in any of his later books. Indeed, he was to complain profoundly in later years of the inability of existing political philosophies, specifically liberalism and Marxism, to provide an analytic framework that could validly cite a goal and the built-in dynamic toward its achievement (liberalism cites voluntary associations as the basis of its pluralist goals, and Marxism cites the working class as the basis of socialism, but neither have been achieved). Although couched as if Mills, the removed social scientist, were describing the model perspective for the "independent Left," it was quite obviously the first statement of Mills's own program. It was an elaborate program, but it rested on sources that revealed something of his earliest political learnings. In his footnotes, he cited G. D. H. Cole, the British socialist, and what he called some "syndicalist literature," such as the internal bulletin of the Johnson-Forrest minority of the American Trotskyist movement. These texts—one by a European radical and the other by a tiny and fragmented American minority—can be taken as suggestive of Mills's long-term inability to find a real "community" of political and social criticism for himself in America. That in 1948 he was possessed of a romantic, though not necessarily unrealistic, identification with workers' movements might best be indicated by the epigraph to his first book. It was from a Nevada worker, who looked back in 1947 and said:

When the boat of wobblies come
Up to Everett, the sheriff says
Don't you come no further
Who the hell's your leader anyhow?
Who's yer leader?
And the wobblies yelled right back—
We ain't got no leader
We're all leaders!
And they kept right on comin!

Mills's program began with the assumption that the Left in America was powerless, distracted, and confused; throughout the world it mostly was losing the struggle for power; and where it was "winning," a hideous Thermidor was being erected. The Main Drift was destructive of the values that historically concerned the Left; it was without significant connection to the broad "sequence of events nor linked securely with large forces of rebellion." Its outlook, then, was a "collective" dream of the impotent. Since there was no existing party Mills wished to address, his declared purpose was to "make the collective dream of the Left manifest." However, his statement of conviction, as it unfolded, clearly indicated a strategy as well as a dream.

The core of the Left's philosophy, to Mills, was humanist and democratic. Society should be organized so that "everyone vitally affected by a social decision, regardless of its sphere, would have a voice in that decision and a hand in its administration.... Left movements have been a series of desperate attempts to uphold the simple values of classic democracy under conditions of giant technology, monopoly capitalism, and the behemoth state—in short, under the conditions of modern life."

This statement should not be construed as *defeatist*—Mills was not among those who accepted an inherent antidemocratic thrust in "the condition of modern life"—but rather as a reflection of *defeat,* the worldwide failure of the Left's vision to be realized in a satisfactory way. Against this tide, Mills advocated a program for the United States based on immediate working-class needs:

- decentralized workers' control at the point of production;
- national social planning, involving all the workers at local and regional levels;
- nationalization, transferring ownership and control from privately organized cliques to make possible the last goal; and
- socialization: "The Left would socialize the means of production in order to further the humanization of man himself. *It is in the workshop, more than in the electoral district, that the new man of a free society must be developed.*"

The Left would insist first and foremost on workers' control so as to transfer power to those who must become "new men" in exercising it. The rest of the "transitional program" toward planning, nationalization, and socialization was to be "a drastic redistribution of real income, accomplished by a sharply graduated income tax, a lifting of indirect consumers' taxation, greatly advanced wages, and greatly reduced price levels."

Since the program was an orthodox one, it was not surprising that Mills suggested two orthodox vehicles for working-class action: the union and the labor party. The union would be the immediate community of the worker, posing the issues that touch his life, pressing to enlarge the democratic power of the worker in the plant, keeping independent of the employer as well as the state.

Independence of Labor action means continual workers' control at the point of production, which means that the union would attempt to replace management function by workers' control at every point where its power permits. The union would proceed as if it were going to become the organizer of work within this society and the basis of social re-organization for a future democratic society.

In order to approximate this situation, organized labor would, first, have to expand its membership to become coextensive with all the people who work for wages and salary; and, second, achieve unity and power behind a program of common interests.

While the union is the key to creating democratic impulse and movement in the shop, the labor party would be the independent political wing having the general purpose of revealing in daily practice "the sovereignty residing in the people." This conception of a silent or unrealized "sovereignty residing in the people" is pivotal to the argument and, as will be seen, tends to vanish—or regress even deeper into dream status, when a few years later Mills virtually declares that the power elite has expropriated the possibility of the people's sovereignty altogether. Here is the labor party in summary:

> The Left would have labor's political party protect, facilitate, and coordinate the struggle for economic and shop democracy, push for a political interlude between wars, in which the distribution of domestic power would have primacy over foreign affairs, prepare the people for a fruitful role in the next slump, establish an intellectual forum and build a public in order that an orderly and continuous re-evaluation of plans and ideas might take place.

Although the Main Drift was more likely to unfold over America, the main chance for arresting and overturning it rested on these factors: the coming slump, the state of the "underdogs" in the lower classes, the "rearguard" forces' potential within the new middle class, and the strategy of the labor leaders and radical intellectuals. It was the first and last time that Mills would indulge in the outlook that later he scorned as a "labor metaphysic" lingering on from the period of Victorian Marxism.

Mills's misreading of the times centered on his expectation of a radicalizing slump: "neither slump nor war will be avoided within the present American system." According to this view, consumer demand, the use of productive capacity, and gross national product would decline after the war-made spurt. In the coming slump and during the "political interlude" prior to the next war, the task of the Left would be to develop a grassroots movement of self-reliant men who would revolt against shop exploitation and fuse into a community-based opposition to prices and rents, organized through consumer cooperatives and linked to the new labor party. Whether this was possible depended for Mills on the readiness of U.S. workers, the unemployed, the small farmers, and certain elements of the middle class. Under slump conditions, he believed the size and significance of these political publics might undergo great change with bewildering swiftness—and "who will catch the people if the system fails them?"

The "aristocracies" of industrial and skilled workers, first, must join ranks with the semi- and unskilled "underdogs"—"those who get the least of what there is to get." Mills recognized among the underdogs certain habits of submission, inabilities to view their problems socially, lack of information as to the nature of their own exploitation, and loss of the power of moral indignation. These are among the very qualities he later used in depicting the lifestyles of the "mass society." Here they remain the socially determined characteristics of a specific subclass. Not only is their style of life related directly to an economic class position, but Mills also suggests and cares about the possibilities for the underdogs to change themselves as a class by changing society. Within a new democratic union community, outside the present system of society, a new type of man can be created who will be able to "shake it to its foundations." Unions and the interlocking labor party, if democratically structured, can "build inside this society something of a new society." This was possible, thought Mills, because the apparent apathy of workers and underdogs was a *deception*. The apathy is realistic; the worker does not want to engage in electoral politics when there are no candidates or issues that deeply concern him. But "the American worker has a high potential militancy when he is pushed, and if he knows what the issue is." This was to be increasingly so; converging with the coming slump, Mills anticipated, is the sudden decline of many of those forces that keep the working class quiescent. The frontier, long a safety valve, was gone. The waves of European migrants, who formerly succeeded each other at the bottom, were no longer coming. Less and less, to Mills, will the new lower classes be able to rationalize their underdog position by comparing it with an even more hideous existence in their historic homelands. In addition, the hollow advertising slogans of the society-in-slump would fool people less and less. All this would take place during a single generation in which already two wars and one slump had occurred. So far these events had not broken down the mentality of acquiescence that rooted itself in the long upward curve from 1870 to 1929 when employment opportunities increased 300 percent and population only 200 percent. But in the coming slump, said Mills, the workers are likely to become insurgent against the society of the slump-war-boom cycle.

But more than workers and underdogs were included in the movement for change that Mills envisioned. Consistent with his faith in the suppressed sovereignty of the people, he was careful to note that "the US public is by no means a compact reactionary mass." He broadened his definition of "common interest" beyond a purely economic category, though leaving the economic category dominant: "All those who suffer the results of irresponsible social decisions and who hold a disproportionately small share of the values available to men in modern society are potential members of the Left." By the time Mills was writing *The Power Elite,* it was precisely this kind of differentiation, between irresponsible decision makers and disadvantaged publics, that was coming to transcend as a crucial notion the economic differentiation between the controllers of the means of production and the employees. In *The New Men of Power,* the two distinctions are merged into a loose concept of social class: Economic position determines roughly the distribution of values. The important members of a labor party, in addition to the workers and underdogs, therefore become the new middle class of salaried employees and the small farmers.

Mills used the term "rearguarders" to describe these new middle classes, to signify that their occupational ideology is politically passive and their tendency is to follow currently dominant forces. In his later *White Collar,* a book that analyzes this "class" in detail, one of Mills's major themes was rearguard politics, but he was considerably more pessimistic by that point about their involvement in any political unity with working people. Moreover, he doubts any political involvement at all on their part, and he makes an analysis of their anxiety in terms that make them more fundamentally part of a "mass society" than a "class society." This kind of explanation is carried further in *The Power Elite,* where "institutional power" and social status factors are more significant than economic class in the distribution of power and the distortion of attitudes in society.

At any rate, the 1948 Mills, still hopeful of an alliance between the underdogs and the rearguarders, stresses that a successful program, if it is to include the new middle classes, must reach out to economic issues, such as prices, that go beyond the wages-and-hours problems of the working people. Thus, he adds, many small farmers, in their struggle for security against the mechanization and surplus of the big corporate farmers, can be linked to urban labor and new middle-class movements where they are organized into consumer cooperatives that fight nationally for price reduction.

Mills came near saying that the greatest obstacle to this program is neither in the social psychology of the classes nor in the stabilized business cycle, but in the organized labor movement. The labor leaders, whom he surveys during three-fourths of the book, are the "new men of power." They derive their status from their inclusion within capitalism as the "responsible" and "cooperative" representatives of the workers. Even the more militant industrial union leaders were becoming respectable, Mills feared, and *lack the militancy of the rank and file.* What is worse, they were oligarchic in their formation, using a variety of measures to dull or put down worker insurgency. Having said this, it is surprising that Mills said nothing in the book about the most pressing union issue of the period: how the CIO should deal with communist and alleged communist influence within its ranks. The history of this period has never fully been written, but now in the 1960s there is increasing evidence that even militant *anti*communists regret the way labor leaders went along with the cold war consensus in refusing to support the right of communists to legitimate roles in the labor movement, subject *only* to constituent workers' consent. Perhaps more than any other organizational factor, the factional dispute over communist participation consumed and internally weakened organized labor in the late 1940s and finalized the incorporation of labor into a pro-American posture for the cold war period. It is therefore odd that Mills, not mentioning this crisis, should go on nevertheless to castigate the "new men of power." They should not toady today, he counseled, to those who would bureaucratize and blunt the movement; they must not capitulate ideologically to those who would bring them into the capitalist consensus. They should not obscure their revolutionary identity by becoming a special interest group. Mills approvingly quoted a *Fortune* editorial that stated that in full political crisis, the middle class first turns to the working class and makes an about turn to the fascist Right only when persuaded that the working class cannot or will not carry through a social revolution.

The conclusion was clear. The way the coming slump affects the workers would determine the future of the labor movement. Current labor leaders, the members of this power elite most vulnerable to displacement pressure, who are incapable of responding to workers' pressure from below, would fall by the way.

This, he declared, is where labor stands: There are labor leaders who are running labor unions, most of them along the Main Drift; there are leftist intellectuals who are not running the unions but who think they know how to run them against the Main Drift; and there are wage workers who are disgruntled and ready to do what must be done. The times were full of possibility. The Main Drift was on its way toward aborting the democratic society, but the slump perhaps would break open a new chance. It depended very much, Mills thought, on what men—workers and intellectuals and labor leaders—were willing to do. Many seemed prepared to move.

Fifteen years later Mills's enthusiasm for the American worker would be dissipated, and though he still criticized the labor leaders, their default alone could not explain away the terrible years of drift. In an especially harsh statement of his views in *The Marxists* (1962), he wrote:

> The revolutionary potential—whatever the phrase may reason-ably mean—of wageworkers, labor unions and political parties, is feeble.... Such facts should not *determine* our view of the future, but they cannot be explained away by references to the corrupt and corrupting "misleaders of labor," to the success of capitalist propaganda, to economic prosperity due to war economy, etc. Assume all this to be true; still the evidence points to the fact that, without serious qualifications, wageworkers under mature capitalism do accept the system. Wherever a labor party exists in an advanced capitalist society, it tends either to become weak or, in actual policy and result, to become incorporated into the welfare state apparatus. Social democratic parties everywhere become merely liberal, a kind of ineffectual, permanent facade of opposition.

The New Men of Power was Mills's last systematic and op-timistic glance at the underdog strata (the poor farmers and industrial unemployed); the working classes; and their allies among the new professionals, managerial and clerical strata, the last a highly more comfortable group but still exploited for the ends of a controlling class. In Mills's work of the 1950s, the underdogs would slide, invisibly, into the mass society. The new middle classes would be there also, without the vantage point, vision, or the means with which to understand and act on their interest. They still would not be a reactionary bloc, excepting the few followers of McCarthy, though they could perhaps become one. For Mills in the 1950s, they were just "inactionary," symbol-izing the larger transition from a political age to one of malaise. It is important to point out this transition, for otherwise the early writings of Mills are lost in stereotyped versions of him as a person only interested in elites. His considered shift away from the 1948 focus easily is forgotten, and with it a realization of Mills's orienting values and perspective, and a sense of the shifting times. Some of the seeds of that shift were evident in the 1948 writing.

Mills was often quite elaborate in 1948 in pointing out status factors, especially among the new labor leaders, that served to cement their aspiration with the Main Drift, to make them gratified at being invited to White House dinners, to turn them against insurgent impulses within the shops where they "got their start." However, these status feelings invariably depend on the class structure for their origin, although Mills is not too clear about the mediating mechanisms, if any, that transmit sentiments of anxiety and aspiration, and images of self from the labor leaders' class position to their consciousness.

Neither is he clear about the mechanisms, such as direct shop revolts, elections, or discussions, by which the rank and file will or will not upset the complacency of the labor leader. At one point, for instance, Mills said that the labor leader is an "organization man" and therefore is capable of fast adjustments depending on pressures; therefore, a workers' protest, caused by slump, would force the labor leader into a more radical role. This point is obscured, though, when Mills indicates that under such conditions *some* leaders will "fall by the way"—which assumes that leaders are more than "organization man," that they are influenced by more complex status pulls. Mills noted earlier the co-opting of labor leaders by the business world, and this perhaps would explain why some leaders will fall by the way. It even might suggest that most of the older, more conservative AFL leaders will most likely "go over" to management in a crisis.

The point of this is that the status analysis is not detailed enough to explain and predict actual social relationships among workers, leaders, and managers within a model of a stagnating political economy. Mills becomes more and more aware of a need to "fill in" these dynamics as his work develops. In later years, again and again he speaks of a need to find the moving links between history and biography; but it is almost as if he enriches the features of the "superstructure" to the neglect of greater attention to class structure. He works out a sophisticated and central distinction between the individual's close-up milieus and the more remote and powerful social structure; he even conceives the power elite itself as a "status group" at one point. As his interest in status enlarges in the 1950s, his interest in class declines.

What also will enlarge in later works is the concept of institutions (aggregates of roles organized for a special purpose) as the dominant expression of human behavior. In *The New Men of Power*, Mills relies on the basic category of "political economy"—essentially meaning property relationships as organized for political and economic purposes. This implicit idea is that institutions, and their commanding elites, are expressions of the political economy, not independent and basic units of society. Therefore, since the political economy is capitalist—that is, owned and controlled by a minority for their profit and aggrandizement—the institutions are shaped and ultimately controlled by capitalist interests. This is true of labor, says Mills, though it need not be if the workers somehow would recognize that neither their economic interest nor their value as self-conscious human beings can be served until the political economy is reorganized.

In addition, capitalism orients the political and economic institutions as well. The politicians are a caste of stabilizers and dealers throughout the world. The military is a caste of protectors and extenders of the capitalist world system. These are the most massive bureaucracies in history, and though their operators do not conform to a pat model of personality or uniform interest, they still are variables dependent on the broad interests of private property. Though this is the logic of his analysis, Mills never develops explicitly a full theory of history, as did Marx, to attempt to show the connection between (1) underlying social structure, which is the root and continuing manner in which people are differentiated by role, function, status, access to resources, and authority, and (2) the proximate, more temporary institutional framework that arises from the differentiation of function. But in *The New Men of Power* he is as close to the theory of *different institutions within capitalist social structure* as he ever will be until the 1960s.

In the next few years, Mills moves from the shadow of Marx to that of Weber: from the view of a single determining economic structure to that of a weighted set of independent institutional orders. His underlying framework is less and less explicit—until the 1960s, when the framework of a capitalist political economy begins to reappear as Mills's definite emphasis, but then without the working class as agency of change. But in the years of Mills's greatest productive outpouring, the power elite, piloting their various institutions, is the primary image of historical dynamics. Whether the unity of industrial, military, and political elites was a function of chance current events and adroit maneuvering, or a function of shared property interests, was a basic question Mills grappled with but left ambiguous in his major works of the 1950s.

Transition: The Puerto Rican Journey

Mills's skepticism deepened rapidly. This was evident a little over one year after *The New Men of Power* in the publication, with Clarence Senior and Rose K. Goldsen, of *The Puerto Rican Journey,* a study of Puerto Rican migrants to New York City. Here Mills continued to anticipate a slump, but more as a question—Can we go much longer expanding?—than as a confident formulation. A slump, of course, would turn American society into a treadmill instead of a ladder for the Puerto Ricans and other new migrants. In addition, Mills wrote, there were other impediments "radicalizing" the Puerto Ricans, such as racial discrimination and a high incidence of unemployable women. However, Mills emphasized the difficulties of protest action occurring on the part of these underdogs. The primary obstacles that Mills saw were psychological:

By living at a similar class level, in the same regions of the city doing the same type of work, having the same type of troubles, being exposed to the same type of mass communications, their imaginative life becomes leveled out. In their day to day struggle, absorbed in the need to function inconspicuously with a minimum of psychic discomfort, they have little time left over for thought about the future.

But where Mills in *The New Men of Power* would point in a balanced way to other psychological factors conducive to protest—underdog hostility to authority, for example—they were largely missing from this analysis, which put the Puerto Rican underdogs in the undifferentiated "lower class mass of the metropolis" (the joining of "class" with "mass" was symbolic of Mills's changing analysis). Furthermore, Mills's attention to unions and parties as agencies of change was revealingly sparse. He devoted less than a page to the East Harlem machine of Congressman Vito Marcantonio. All he wrote was that Marcantonio found genuine as well as contrived means of identifying with the people—and that he would continue to flourish "until other community organizations competitively succeed in servicing the needs of the migrants." As for the unions, he pointed out that a large number of Puerto Ricans—51 percent—were organized already, particularly into locals of the International Ladies Garment Workers' Union (ILGWU). He does not discuss the potential for economic and political change—if any—implicit in this fact, nor does he ask why *unionized* Puerto Ricans still remain in the underdog stratum.

It is important to examine what Mills did *not* say about Marcantonio and the ILGWU, for it suggests a picture of the changes taking place in American society from 1946 to 1953. First, there *was* a facsimile labor party, the American Labor Party (ALP), which had grown out of the Non-Partisan League in 1936. To Mills, writing in *The New Men of Power,* it was "not a party but a tactical device of the New Deal to promote its own political fortunes in New York." By the 1940s, however, the ALP was supported by left-wing unionists, independent radicals, and the Communist Party, as well as masses of New York Puerto Ricans. Marcantonio was its greatest public representative. When Mills was writing, the ALP was under tremendous fire from all the elements that had opposed the 1948 Progressive Party campaign of former commerce secretary Henry Wallace. One of the leading forces fighting the ALP was the ILGWU, which long has served as a major coordinator of the "liberal-labor [anti-communist] community." In 1950, in order to defeat Marcantonio, the Liberal, Democratic, and Republican parties coalesced behind a single candidate, James Donovan; even though Marcantonio lost the race, he ran ahead of the vote given any of the three individual parties. This coalition, after defeating Marcantonio, did not build the kind of grassroots community organization Mills said was needed. Indeed, the miserable problems and politics of Spanish Harlem remained virtually unchanged until the late 1950s when new insurgents, from part of the ALP tradition, arose to defeat the regular incumbent and make partial gains for the Puerto Rican community.

What is astonishing about Mills's reference to the ALP and the ILGWU is the turnaround from his references to them in *The New Men of Power*. In the first book, Mills described the ALP *critically* as an instrument for advancing the interests of the New Deal, giving opportunist labor leaders the chance to keep their ties to the Democratic Party from the 1930s while still upholding the traditional rhetoric of "independent labor action." The ILGWU is the very union Mills singled out in *The New Men of Power* as representative of this tendency. It was, to Mills, a union that traveled from a socialist to an establishment identity, under the leadership of David Dubinsky. Mills did not point out, as did Herbert Hill, labor secretary of the National Association for the Advancement of Colored People (NAACP) in 1960, that the ILGWU also was anti–Puerto Rican in its wage and leadership policies although the bulk of its members were Puerto Rican. Had he lived, Mills would also have seen, in 1963 and 1964, Negro and Puerto Rican leaders from the Marcantonio period returning to help lead mass movements against high rents and segregated inferior education in New York City.

This is not the place to inquire of Mills's personal and political associations at that time, although that discussion probably would be necessary to fully understand this shift. However, it is a picture of the master trends that we seek in this study of Mills's work. The main point, therefore, is not why Mills the man became disappointed in the industrial workers and underdogs so quickly, or why he wrote neutrally of organizations where once he was vehemently critical. The main point is that the lower classes were "abandoned" not simply by Mills but by all the organizations that professed to speak for the lower classes. This finally included the American Communist Party, which left Marcantonio and returned to the folds of the Democratic Party under the pretext of "not dividing from the masses."

This shift in Mills's analysis cannot be explained in terms of a deepening sophistication about underdog psychology. Although it is clear that he recognizes more subtle qualities of individual character in the book, he takes a different general view of characters as well. This different view did not imply a change in Mills's values, either: he cared as much about democracy but was more dubious about its prospect. To achieve an understanding of the shift, which became much more pronounced in his work of the mid-1950s, it is necessary to see the changing character of U.S. life, politics, and economy in the dramatic ten years after World War II. The slump *did* come, but it was absorbed in a kind of *stabilization* of Western societies that Mills did not anticipate fully in the 1940s. This stabilization became perhaps the crucial factor allowing the rise of the power elite, but Mills did not recognize it as it happened, at least not until the early 1960s—and then he elevated it to a fundamental principle just at a time, as we shall see, when Western societies, especially the United States, seemed to be passing from stability to a condition of enlarging tremor again. To envision the unfolding of these structural and social crises, it is necessary to begin with the event of stabilization and the slump that came unfelt.

The Strategy of Stabilization

What Mills observed in the immediate postwar years confirmed much that he feared—the sophisticated conservative strategy was working. There is no doubt that many American leaders expected a severe postwar recession primarily due to armaments cutbacks. Instead, there was an amazing boom, raising gross national product (in 1960 dollars) from $100 million in 1940 to $213 million in 1945 to $284 million in 1950. The basic elements in the boom were the buildup of consumer needs, purchasing power, and corporation investment capital; the basic strategy for the boom consisted in expanded overseas trade and the permanent war economy—and the Korean War "clinched" the maintenance of the boom.

During ten years of depression, about four-fifths of American families received an average cash income under $2,000. "I see millions of families trying to live on incomes so meager that the pall of family disaster hangs over them day by day. I see one-third of a nation ill-housed, ill-clothed, ill-fed" is the way FDR *under*stated the problem in 1937. During the Depression few people spent on homes, automobiles, or other normal consumer items. Even at the end of the 1930s, there seemed no relief in prospect for the ten million unemployed and the millions of other insecure individuals and families.

Then, of course, came World War II and with it the drastic enlargement of employment opportunities. The poor industrial workers, farmers, and even the underdogs, most notably the Negroes who had migrated North, went back to the assembly lines. There they quickly earned more money than they could accumulate during the entire decade of the 1930s. Everyone worked, and many worked overtime. However, the austerity in spending continued through the war years while wide anxiety prevailed—in fact, the total purchases of houses, automobiles, refrigerators, and other durables were lower during the war years than the depression years. The result at war's end was a fantastic spree to secure the comforts that had been denied for a full fifteen years.

The spree was possible because of the stored-up purchasing power accumulated especially during the war. Between 1929 and the mid-1930s, total individual savings fluctuated between $41 and $48 billion; in 1940, they reached $59 billion; at the end of the war, they totaled a tremendous *$135 billion,* or about one-quarter of gross individual earnings. Compensation in income to employees *doubled* between 1940 and 1945, and the 1945 amount was over *four times* the 1933 depression low. The studies of Gabriel Kolko indicate that there was no fundamental redistribution of income across the "income-tenths" into which he divides the population. However, this perpetuation of income inequality was an old fact of life in America; the new fact for most Americans was the *more affluent inequality* enjoyed after the long period of war and depression.

With this accumulated purchasing power, American consumers plunged forward to make the boom. In fact, they went all out: total short- and intermediate-term consumer credit standing was $5.6 million in 1945, $11.6 million in 1947, and $17.3 million by 1949. Former critics of the economy watched in awe. Former apologists gasped in pride.

The big corporations created immense inventories and savings during the same fifteen years, 1929 through 1944. The 1945 profit level doubled that of 1940, and by 1950 it was doubled again. Simultaneous with consumer austerity, the corporations had experienced fifteen years of little spending for equipment, plant, and factories. By the end of the war, they were overweighted with capital and investment plans. Much of their wartime research and design, financed largely by $306 billion in government contracts between 1942 and 1946, and developed in greater tandem with the military than at any time since the eighteenth century, led in two vital directions The first was toward world competitive leadership, and the second toward the automation of the economy; but the latter would not be felt until the former trend was coming to a halt.

The boom was not an explosion of natural market forces. A conscious strategy was at work. How to avoid a new slump and its attendant crisis—that was the question that *Fortune, Business Week,* and other organs of corporate thought were asking. Among the solutions that the conservatives would have preferred forgotten were, first, deficit spending on public works and, second, the direct or indirect subsidization of income. From a business viewpoint, the first of these proposals would set a "socialist" precedent, with lower profit rates, and involve the government in direct competition with private industry in such sectors as housing and school construction. The second would contradict the ethos of capitalism by furthering the welfare state "revolution." The alternative was to look beyond American boundaries to overseas markets. Assistance and loan programs to other nations would pump up the world market and, as the editors of *Fortune* then indicated, "nine-tenths of the money loaned would be spent in the US for US goods ... it has no place else to go."

President Truman concurred in this viewpoint; for instance, his midyear 1949 Economic Report declared that "the expansion of foreign investment will improve the rest of the world's ability to buy from us." (This orientation still prevails, of course; in 1963, 80 percent of the congressional foreign aid appropriation was spent in the Untied States.) *Business Week* chimed in, too, saying in January 1948 that the maintenance of full employment in America would require that "our total export volume must be about three times that of the years just before World War II. Our exports of machinery must be about five times greater."

Even before the war had ended, American statesmen, industrialists, and labor leaders were concerned about the exports question. Few voiced disagreement with the 1944 testimony of Dean Acheson before a special subcommittee of the Congressional Committee on Postwar Economic Policy and Planning. Acheson shunned the alternative of a publicly owned economy and spelled out the policy consequences of the choice to go on with private enterprise:

> If you wish to control the entire trade and income of the United States, which means the life of the people, you could probably fix

it so that everything produced here would be consumed here, but that would completely change our constitution, our relations to property, human liberty, our own very conceptions of law. And nobody contemplates that. Therefore, you find you must look to other markets and those markets are abroad.... We need these markets for the output of the United States. If I am wrong about that, then all the argument falls by the wayside, but my contention is that we cannot have full employment and prosperity in the United States without foreign markets.... How do we go about getting it? What you have to do at the outset is make credit available.... I don't believe private capital can possibly do it.... I don't think there is enough private capital willing to engage in that activity, which is quite risky. There will be a lot of losses.

So began what Mills called the "New Deal on a world basis." American exports showed a favorable balance almost everywhere in 1929: about 17 percent of world exports originated in the United States. But by the end of the Depression, despite FDR's subsidies and loans and his 1935 claim that "foreign markets must be regained if America's producers are to rebuild a full and enduring domestic prosperity," the American share dropped to under 15 percent.

During the war, tension about the markets problem became manifest, and massive government subsidies permitted industry to do the research and development that might lead to lower-cost export goods after the war. This process, along with war-produced surpluses, joined historically with the tremendous needs of a war-devastated Europe to effect a fast expansion of U.S. trade in the late 1940s. As a study sponsored by the Council on Foreign Relations declared positively in the mid-1950s, total U.S. investment overseas in the years 1946–1955 sped from $18.7 billion to $44.9 billion, including $19.2 billion in long-term direct private investment. Of this last amount, $6.5 billion went to Canada, $6.6 billion to Latin America, $3 billion to Western Europe, and over $3 billion to other areas. However, it was not until 1956 that the U.S. export level, minus government subsidies, recaptured its 1929 share in the world economy.

The 1947 Marshall Plan was the economic blueprint for this establishment of U.S. hegemony in trade by pumping up the ravaged sister countries. The economic motive was not the only one expressed—some, like Marshall himself, in his famous Harvard speech, stressed humanitarian purposes; others stated flatly the need to shore up European countries against the threat of left-wing movements or the Russian Army. A guerilla struggle in Greece already was under way; the Left in Italy and France seemed extraordinarily powerful; the Red Army seemed poised on the European border. These several reasons were compatible, and they stemmed from a defense of the private economy as the keystone of Western freedom. Marshall added the economic argument to the humanitarian one when he told Congress in 1947 that unless the plan was adopted, "The cumulative loss of foreign markets and sources of supply would unquestionably have a depressing influence on our domestic economy and would drive us to increased measures of government control." But exports alone would not guarantee economic security, or so the leaders believed. In the growing conflict with the Soviet Union, there was ample justification for a new pump primer: a war economy carried into peacetime, safe for sophisticated conservatism.

General Electric's Charles Wilson called it the "permanent war economy." It was justified for political-military reasons. By 1945, Russian-American relations were breaking down; by 1946, a "hard" administration fired the "soft" Commerce Secretary Wallace after his Madison Square Garden speech advocating coexistence. The Truman Plan, finally delivered to Congress in March 1947, two months prior to the Marshall Plan, committed the United States to "support free peoples who are resisting attempted subjugation by armed minorities or outside pressure." The United States was beginning the buildup of a world system of military alliances—first, to prevent social revolution and, second, to enforce the influential "containment" theory of George Kennan, former ambassador to Russia who became a key cold war strategist in the Department of State. The terms of this doctrine, with its curious echoes of the accepted Acheson thesis on foreign markets, interpreted the Soviet Union as inherently requiring expansion to preserve its domestic power structure. Therefore, a world ring of military defense, backed by an alert and mobilized America, was the expected apparatus that would protect investment and eventuate in Russian collapse.

The assumption here is that these political and military doctrines represented the sincere feelings of the political, military, and economic personnel who shaped American postwar foreign policy. However, it is compatible with the thesis of their sincerity to point out the profound ways in which the enveloping cold war served to prolong the elite role played by the hundreds of individuals linked together in the superorganizations that planned and operated World War II. In particular, it is crucial to see the domestic economic consequences. It meant that while America brought home its troops and demilitarized a considerable part of its productive system following the war, the defense economy and its cluster of industries never returned to prewar levels. The percentage of defense spending in overall federal budgeting was 20 percent in 1940, averaged about 80 percent in the war years, but averaged about 35 percent for five years until the Korean War shot it to the 60 percent level. Even the 35 percent figure is somewhat deceptive since it neglects *projected* defense expenditure.

In 1948, Mills anticipated much of this development.

> The conservative way to economic balance, without disturbing the income and power relations between the classes, is deficit spending in foreign rather than in domestic fields, coupled with building a war economy in time of peace. Even the greatest conceivable expansion of foreign markets in the world today would not alone begin to neutralize the economic factors that are making for slump. The two go together in the American constellation of monopoly power.

Mills made brief references to the rise of the military and its neat conjunction with the business community—a theme he would take up elaborately in *The Power Elite.* What he saw was capitalism in crisis: dragged into utopian policies such as the abolition of labor unions, which, to the extent implemented, causes a slump because of the declining purchasing power in the lower classes; dragged by "sophisticated conservatives" into an insistent Open Door Policy abroad and a war economy at home; finally, pulling out of the cycle of slump and war into a corporate state ruling a militarized society. In a grim prophecy, he anticipated the way in which the cold war would require a consolidation of power and the destruction of social relationships characteristic of a free society: "When the military state is joined with private monopoly power, a permanent war economy is required to maintain the productive apparatus in a condition of profitable utilization and society in a *state of acquiescent dread.*"

Would this be sufficient to roll back the slump tendencies inherent in the economy? The question became moot because of the Korean War. However, prior to the war, there were indications that a slump was under way.

The 1948–1950 slump was the first, and mildest, of the four in the postwar period. Business investment started to fall in 1948, dropping nearly $10 billion by the second quarter of 1949, and accounting for a 3.6 percent slip in gross national product from $266 billion in 1948 to $256 billion at the trough or recession. The federal government dropped from an operating surplus of nearly $4 billion to a deficit of the same amount six months later. Unemployment increased from 3.7 percent of the labor force to as much as 7 percent by the end of 1948. These circumstances were officially unnoticed during most of the period. The fear continued to be of an inflationary spiral, as it had been since the war years. The Council of Economic Advisers, perhaps for political reasons as well as because of an insufficient amount of data, failed to note the recession until its April 1949 report. In that document the council mildly advanced the thesis that a business downturn was a greater possibility than inflation unless there were "healthy price adjustments with only moderate temporary departures from maximum levels of employment and production." There was not even administration unity on this theme. Secretary of the Treasury John Snyder, as much as a year later, was informing the public that *all* the postwar years were prosperous ones.

A Brookings Institution study concluded that "the backlogs of demand for automobiles and housing were still large, and both of those played an important role in the mildness of the recession." Defense spending was not fundamentally important as a stabilizer, according to the same study—though it absorbed 35 percent of public sector outlay, and the Council of Economic Advisers was becoming "heavily involved" with planning for defense. Recovery came in the months just before the June 1950 explosion of war in Korea. The war absorbed the unemployed, whose numbers had declined but little (to 5.3 percent) by spring 1950. Although numerous attitude polls during the early 1950s indicated an antiwar weariness among the American people, the mood did not carry over to the economic system, which achieved full employment only during war. Indeed, a general enthusiasm continued to rise, shored up by the increased income and savings created in the war period.

In short, the slump had come, but nearly unnoticed. A recovery began, except in the area of unemployment, and quickly accelerated in the Korean War period. Elites in almost every field felt a confidence and often an astonishment at capitalism's recovery. The system that many had denounced or worried over a decade before was now seemingly more productive than it ever had been. A new folklore of capitalism sprang up, and new balconies of comfort for the social reformers of the 1930s. Those who believed the prosperity was fake or immoral went unheard—except perhaps by the McCarthyist movement that isolated them further. These years marked the end of radical hopes that stayed burning in the 1940s and the beginning of a long conservative rule. The system had been stabilized—or so it seemed to Mills.

Chapter 2

The Power Elite and the Mass Society

The Theory of the Power Elite

*T*HE *POWER ELITE* WAS THE MAJOR EXPRESSION OF MILLS'S theory of American social structure and power relationships; he insisted until the end of his life that, with very few modifications, it was a valid explanation of the society in which he lived. However, in accepting the continuity of this theory, we are likely to be insensitive to the particular ways in which the book, like all of Mills's work, "fit" the time in which it was written.

Postwar Changes

First, the Korean War not only erased the slump but lifted U.S. society to new heights of prosperity. The wages and savings of the industrial workforce rose with the general uplift of the labor force. Even the more repressed minorities, in particular the Negroes, benefited from the migration to northern cities where work opportunities opened up in war industries. Today it is quite often acknowledged—by economists Herman Miller and Gabriel Kolko, for example—that these postwar economic gains were *not* part of a major redistribution of wealth in America following the New Deal but rather a continuation of long-term income distribution trends. That is, the *relative* position of the working class remained the same in society, although the working-class individual experienced an absolute income increase due to the general national upswing. For the Negro, there actually were small relative as well as absolute gains in the 1940s. But these were explainable in the main by the migration to northern urban centers where wage levels ordinarily are higher than in the South. In other words, the Negro, too, remained in the same relative position—at or near the bottom—in his specific place of work although he made a relative gain on the national level. These subtleties mostly went unnoticed, however, as intellectuals tended to greet the postwar society with applause for what Simon Kuznets and others called its peaceful "income revolution." These moods certainly were not congenial to social criticism or the atmosphere in which a Left could be invigorated.

McCarthyism added to the depletion of Left influence. Its development, from 1951 to 1953, was not merely a two-year burst of reaction but reflected the widespread suspicion of free association and its alleged consequence—communist infiltration that had been building up for some time, since well before World War II—and not only within conservative but liberal ranks as well. At few times in American history has there been less effective protest against ruling policy than in the early 1950s.

The possibilities of protest evaporated, also, through the internal dynamics of factionalism within the socialist and communist movements. As the void developed on the Left, and as a reactionary din sounded in Congress and through local American society, however, something else was developing at the higher levels of policymaking.

The Korean War was not only an economic convenience. Its other key function was to hoist the military into stable power and put the nation on a continuous war footing. The velocity at which this proceeded was phenomenal. The military had received recognition as an independent "peacetime" institution in 1947. The cold war, which members of the military participated in creating, legitimated their ongoing development. But it was the confrontation in Korea that reinforced not only the national expectation of permanent war and cold war, but permanent military participation in public affairs as well.

The rapid ascendance of a military elite brought it into working linkage with the corporations. The cold war imagery of the Free World against the Communist Conspiracy was descending on the nation, and the dissenting function of the Left was devastated.

Congress was "outmoded" in the new order of things. Hardly organized to deal with foreign policy, it was structurally unprepared for the radical shift of crisis from the domestic to the international scene. Never organized to regulate capitalist oligopoly in an urban industrial society, it either became a place of small-business outcry or an acquiescent part of the new corporate order. This especially was true of the House of Representatives, where rural and southern overrepresentation persists, and the seniority system and cunning strategies have kept a conservative coalition of southern Democrats and midwestern Republicans in control of legislation and patronage since the 1930s.

This series of changes in American social structure and social psychology were reflected in and, to some degree, explain, *The Power Elite*. It was at once Mills's brilliant move, and perhaps his most important error, to take these sudden changes to be indicative of the coming long-term organization of American society.

Historical Portraits of the Elite

Mills's conception was that the power elite signified the beginning of a fifth historical epoch in the ordering of power relations in the United States. Mills's history was not one of capitalist development continuously shaping the governing and other institutions of society. It was a more ambivalent history, taking into account the shifting relations of political, economic, and military orders, a study symbolic in many ways, as we shall see, of the theoretical dilemmas at the heart of the power elite concept.

The first epoch of power wielding, for Mills, ran roughly from the time of the American Revolution to the presidency of John Quincy Adams, and it was marked by a tight coincidence of military, economic, and political orders, overseen by an interlocked and personally acquainted elite. This form of minority control, however, was broken in the second epoch from the "Jeffersonian revolution" to the Civil War. In those three-quarters of a century, power was dispersed more widely than in any previous or later time. The "loose" social structure was due to the rapid expansion of land-owning opportunity, simultaneous with the Jacksonian uplifting of the "common man." The economic order, to Mills, "was ascendant over both social status and political power; within the economic order, a quite sizeable proportion of all the economic men were among those who decided." Division opened in the economic order and, according to Mills, resulted in the Civil War. At this point the union, with a national economy, was firmly established and quickly centered on the private corporation as its institutional form. Rising out of the processes of national industrialization, the corporation signaled the end of the broad dispersal of power insofar as it had depended on widespread property ownership in either agriculture or manufacturing. Where three-quarters of the population had worked their own property, the new society would consolidate property into a corporate form owned and controlled by a small minority. This third epoch, from 1866 until the 1929 crash, was that of supremacy for finance capitalism; political and military power was steered to economic ends, often with blatant and crass techniques.

The 1929 crash began the fourth epoch, one that involved competing centers of power in the economic and political orders. The New Deal was a time of shifting balances: the power of business "was not replaced, but it was contested and supplemented; it became one major power within a structure of power that was chiefly run by political men and not by economic or military men turned political." It was here, perhaps, that the major flaws in this variety of history telling can be seen. In stressing the division of history into epochs, it necessarily understressed two phenomena. The first is historical *continuity,* such as the long-term consensus favoring private property and possessive individualism, which coexists with historical *discontinuity,* such as the shifts from an agrarian to an industrial nonunion to a unionized economy. The implication of this continuity seems to be that American institutional development has served the changing needs of a maturing capitalism. The second phenomenon understressed is the dynamic period, so to speak, "between" epochs: there is no sense in Mills's history of the generative forces that develop in one epoch and become dominant in a later one. (Thus, he adopts the fallacy that corporation capitalism began only during and after the Civil War, whereas its origins were prior to, and partially precipitated, the war.)

In Mills's writing it is almost as if political, economic, and military groups are "jockeying" for position or that their respective institutional orders rise or fall contingent merely on "changing conditions." Thus, the New Deal appears almost as a spasm response by political men, previously waiting in the wings of history, to the default of economic men. This would be a fair characterization were it not for the persistent ambiguity in Mills's work since, on the other hand, he realizes the "New Deal saved capitalism," a thesis that suggests some kind of overarching role in society for capitalist institutions and values. The conclusion from this perspective, however, would not be that "distinctly political" men were dominant but that capitalism-in-crisis needed political tools to stabilize and recover. The dominance of capitalist consensus therefore could be inferred from the fact that it prevailed during and after its period of greatest weakness. Mills does not go this far, although the hint of this is certainly evident and inescapable in his economic interpretation of the New Deal. The theoretical emphasis on separate and independent institutional orders prevails over that of a comprehensive capitalist institutional structure, and with this emphasis Mills goes on to develop his famous theory of the power elite.

The context for this new elite is the fifth epoch, which began with World War II. The essential mechanics of the epoch, to Mills, were as follows:

- The decline of politics as a major professional role, and the greatly enlarged direct domination of government by other institutional hierarchies in combination with political "outsiders" who had matured in nonpolitical roles.
- A "new point of explicitness" in business-government partnership. During the New Deal, the corporation chieftains joined the political directorate; as of World War II, they have come to dominate it.
- A "military ascendancy" to "decisive political relevance." This rise was due, said Mills, to a new and pivotal fact in U.S. history: "The focus of elite attention has been shifted from domestic problems, centered in the '30s around slump, to international problems, centered in the '40s around war." In these circumstances, the military would benefit most. With authority derived from the military character of the times and granted by other American policymakers, the military moved into the "vacuum" in foreign policy decision making. This vacuum stemmed also from the absence of any historical political agencies suitable to deal extensively with foreign and military problems.
- An economy configured by high defense outlays and private corporate power. American capitalism is now in considerable part a military capitalism, and the most important relationships of the big corporations to the state rest on the coincidence of interests between military and corporate needs, as defined by warlords and corporate rich.

The American Attitude toward Power

Ideas of this sort are not widely shared in the United States. From the colonial period to the present day, Americans have tended to see power as a dangerous thing, inherently corrupting and expansive for the user. John Adams's eighteenth-century assertion of a negative view of power is still fashionable today: "Power naturally grows ... because human passions are insatiable. But that power alone can grow which already is too great; that which is unchecked; that which has not power to control it." This mood stemmed not only from the colonists' experience with continental tyranny but also of course from upper-class fears of the agrarian dirt farmers and urban "mobs" beginning to develop in the colonies. It stemmed as well from traditional debates about British constitutionalism, but perhaps the more important ideological tradition in forming this view of power was that of Puritanism. When depravity is seen at the core of personality, it is logical to emphasize the need for maximum restraint on the ability of individuals to gain and use power. If men incorrigibly pursue a selfish interest, even where they must plunder others to succeed in their pursuit, then an institutional framework of checks and balances seems a rational way to organize society. Though most class-conscious colonials feared the power of the propertyless masses and saw the central state as a means toward a stable national economy, there also was apprehension about the use of monopoly power *within* upper-class circles. The conservative governor Morris of Virginia, for instance, said at the Constitutional Convention that "wealth tends to corrupt the mind and to nourish its love of power and to stimulate it to oppression. History proves this to be the spirit of the opulent."

The development of institutions to embody the fear of power was accompanied by other developments that suggested that oppression was not a real possibility in the "unique" American circumstances. The chief influence of this sort was the expanding frontier of the nineteenth century that seemed to offer limitless opportunities for wealth, freedom, and power. Madison, it might be noted, had realized this possibility in the eighteenth century and pointed to it as one of the chief means by which class conflicts could be dissipated. These tendencies did not fully obscure the use of naked power, but in those periods when such power was rather obviously corroding democratic institutions, there always appeared indignant and *apparently* effective attacks on monopoly power (the reform movements of agrarian radicals, abolitionists, populists, muckrakers, progressives, trade unionists, socialists, and today the Negroes). In the twentieth century, especially since 1940, so many agencies have developed as supposed counterforces to corporation power that it may be virtually impossible for most Americans to conceive of a freely ruling economic class.

And while the existence of an *elite* has been obscured, there has developed also an ideology of power and democracy emphasizing limitations on *popular* participation and control. A federal system was seen as indispensable to maintaining order; indirect representation would remove the statesmen from their less sophisticated constituencies; the checks and balances would frustrate the chance for rule by a narrow-interest group; the public sphere was limited specifically by the warning that "that government which governs least governs best." Through all of American history, social thought has been distinguished by these dominant themes. A historian of ideas could find fascinating lines from market economics to modern theories of countervailing power; from Federalist Paper No. 10 to the political theory of liberal pluralism; from de Tocqueville's vision of voluntary associations to modern theories of social equilibrium; from Puritanism to the modern skeptical and "neo-orthodox" philosophies; from the fears of mob rule to the fears of mass society; and so on.

Whatever its setting and whatever its formulation, it is undeniably true that a negative view of power, especially where that power is to be placed in state machinery, still prevails among most Americans. Power in society is seen to flow back and forth between the government, corporations, labor unions, and other colossal institutions. It is still the world of Adam Smith, but the invisibly balanced atomic units are large-scale institutions rather than individual enterprises. The endless, shifting balances supposedly permit individuals a relative freedom to act or to be private, and a guarantee against the seizure of power by any single class or institutional order. The chief fear usually is that the control of economics and politics not fall into one set of hands: "that is what happened in the Soviet Union, and it must not happen here." To guarantee that it not happen here, the argument goes, the separate corporations should remain free to profit and invest; the government should set some limits on the concentration of power but should itself be limited only to actions that do not interfere with the corporate freedom to plan and invest privately.

In a certain sense, Mills's dissent from this ideological mainstream was not new, for there always has been a minority current. From the agrarian and urban radicals of the eighteenth century down through the abolitionists, populists, and socialists, there flows an attack on power as the privilege of elites, and an advocacy that power instead be a resource of society widely and publicly used. To be sure, there are fundamental differences within this dissenting tradition, specifically those between the laissez-faire and socialist points of view, but it is nevertheless a tradition with a common bias toward "the people" and against privilege. "The mass" is not so feared as "the elite." Public and open power is not so feared as the ratification of private power wielding. The expectation is that men are capable of using power to achieve worthy purposes.

The 1930s resounded with the rhetoric of dissent but began and ended with the almost invisible fact of entrenched private power. By the 1940s and 1950s, there was little left but the echoes of the old anger, as a kind of memento of a time permanently past. Thus, while Mills in one sense was heir to a long protest tradition (he identified, for example, with Marx and Veblen), in terms of his immediate situation he was intellectually isolated. Almost nowhere in America, during the years Mills wrote, were there writers and thinkers who shared his sense of inquiry and his imagery of power. The 1950s were a time of resurgence for neo-Madisonian thought; the equilibrium sociology of Talcott Parsons and the veto-group theories of David Riesman were, for example, two of the representative themes that welded a high intellectual consensus. Another example was the publication of *The New American Right,* a collection of essays by some of the most prolific social critics in the United States, including Parsons and Riesman, who defined stratification in status, rather than class, terms and interpreted the McCarthyites in terms of status anxieties in the midst of an otherwise progressive social order.

The Theory of the Elite

Into this heavy atmosphere Mills fired his dramatic symbol of minority rule; he dismissed the "balanced society" viewpoint as merely descriptive of the "middle levels of power." He took the diamond-shaped income distribution model and set it within a pyramid-shaped model of power distribution (see diagram below).

As will be seen, Mills himself overstated the degree to which income had been actually redistributed; he interpreted the "upsurge" of the 1940s as a trend that would last, whereas it was in fact a temporary shift that never basically altered the twenty-five-year trend of income distribution.

Dominant popular misgivings, and academic criticism, of Mills's conception usually stress that the existence of a power elite is impossible because, first, it assumes a cabal or conspiracy able to master a wide scope of actions and, second, a conscious

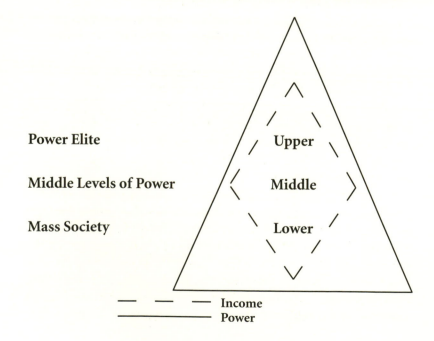

Power Elite

Middle Levels of Power

Mass Society

Upper

Middle

Lower

— — — Income
———— Power

unity of programmatic interest among the nation's leadership. There are other critiques, to be sure, but these tend to be the most serious and orthodox, adopted in whole or part by Bell, Lipset, Parsons, Dahl, Schlesinger, and others. Mills contended with these views by taking a position that *avoided* both assumptions. Meisel and others have pointed out his unusual form of elite theory in which the assumptions of consciousness, cohesion, and conspiracy are avoided by assumptions about institutional integration. His own summary is incisive:

> Within the elite as a whole this coincidence of interest between the high military and the corporate chieftains strengthens both of them and further subordinates the role of the merely political men. Not politicians but corporate executives sit with the military and plan the organization of the war effort.... The military capitalism of private corporations exists in a weakened and formal democratic system containing a military order already quite political in outlook and demands. Accordingly, at the top of this structure, the power elite has been shaped by the coincidence of interest between those who control the major means of production and those who control the newly-enlarged means of violence; from the decline of the professional politician and the rise of explicit political command of the corporation chieftains and military warlords; from the absence of any genuine civil service of skill and integrity, independent of vested interests.

His argument, formally summarized, was

1. There is a high correspondence of interests among large institutional hierarchies.
2. The interests of these institutions in general are complementary and sometimes identical.
3. The personnel of these institutions are quite alike; from the upper-third in income distribution; Americans by birth; the descendents of businessmen; urban; most often from the east; inclined to similar status codes; oriented to amassing power, wealth, or prestige. Many know each other with some

agreeable familiarity, due to their joint experience on war production boards, trade associations or government agencies, or their common pursuits of sport or culture. Some, though fewer and fewer, know each other through linked family backgrounds.

4. Each of these institutional centers can be considered independent and able to cause social change.

5. Behind these developments, and accelerated by them, are long-term pressures: first, toward rationalization inherent in industrial society; second, toward the integration of a threatened social system for the purposes of defense.

The problem of verifying this thesis is one of the more controversial and well-trodden ones in the discussion of Mills. If the elite is approached from the perspective of common class and social backgrounds, only limited headway is made. It can be established, for example, that the members of the three elites are from roughly compatible, though hardly similar, business or professional class origins. It can be established, further, that each domain is undergoing forms of bureaucratization that demand homogenous behavior among their own personnel; and, finally, that each institutionalized elite develops major points of compatibility with the other. To begin with information about social origins, Suzanne Keller's recent summary of existing research on American elites is quite incisive and helpful in that it includes several elite categories in addition to those Mills used (see tables 2.1–2.5, based on Keller's charts).

But these crude similarities, it has been argued, do not constitute proof of any kind of ruling elite. Arthur Schlesinger's criticism of Mills, for instance, argues that "the power elite" concept connotes a conspiracy for which there is no evidence. A more elaborate argument by Robert Dahl claims that Mills gives wholly insufficient evidence, in terms of actual historical decisions, to verify the claim of a power elite, with comprehensive policymaking scope, that actually uses its power. It is largely true that Mills's work contains few concrete case studies of decisions,

Table 2.1 Nativity

Strategic Elite	Percentage of Foreign Born	Percentage of Second Generation
Political	2	15
Military	2	9 (West Point class of 1960)
Diplomatic	4	8
Business	6	18
Film	25	No information

Note: The majority of foreign-born and second-generation came from northwest Europe.

Table 2.2 Rural-Urban Origins

Strategic Elite	Percentage of Urban Born (in towns of 2,500 or more)
Political	48
Journalistic	61
Diplomatic	66
Business	65
Military	30–40*

*Taking U.S. Army, Navy, and Air Force separately.

Table 2.3 Religious Affiliation

Strategic Elite	Percentage of Protestant
Diplomatic	60
Journalistic	70
Political	81
Business	85
Military	90

but, while this gap is unfortunate, it is as equally beside the point as Schlesinger's charge of a conspiracy thesis. In both cases, the critics miss Mills's most fundamental argument: that the power elite rests on the tendencies and directions of complementary institutional growth. This perspective allows him to make the

Table 2.4 Father's Occupation

Strategic Elite	Percentage of Professional
Business	15
Political	24
Higher civil servants	28
Diplomatic	32
Journalistic	43
Military	
U.S. Air Force	38
U.S. Army	45
U.S. Navy	45
Film	50

Strategic Elite	Percentage of Proprietary and Official
Journalistic	24
Military	29
Higher civil servants	26
Film	33
Political	35
Diplomatic	36
Business	57

Strategic Elite	Percentage of Farmers
Film	4
Diplomatic	6
Journalistic	9
Military	10
Business	15
Higher civil servants	29
Political	32

Strategic Elite	Percentage of Wage Earners
Diplomatic	3
Military	5
Political	5
Film	5
Higher civil servants	10
Journalistic	11
Business	15

Table 2.5 Educational Attainment

Strategic Elite	Percentage of College Graduates
Film (1930s)	18
Journalistic	52
Business	61
Higher civil servants	80
Diplomatic	81
Military	
U.S. Air Force	73
U.S. Army	85
U.S. Navy	98
Political	91

argument that the power elite can exist without being conspiratorial, conflict-free, or organized. Thus visible decision-making groups such as Congress, small businessmen, farmers—and "local society" in general—which occupy so much of the active and communicative attention of the society, can be seen as groups that are subordinate to less visible ones "at the top." At the same time, debates between the State Department and the Joint Chiefs of Staff over Southeast Asia policy, no matter how bitter, are debates between groups united at a deeper level. That is, if Mills had cared to use the case technique for verifying his theory, it would not have been simply an attempt to show where and how "the public" was shut out of various key decisions. Rather, he probably would have pointed to the agreed-on consensus underlying the debates that occurred—the main points of consensus favoring private corporate property and anticommunism. This research has yet to be done (long ago the American Left retired from serious research). But even cursory reflection on some major postwar decisions would suggest that Mills was right about the character of the underlying consensus and, certainly with respect to the international decisions, the relative immunity of the elites from public review:

> Defense procurement policies in World War II
> The reconversion decisions after the war
> The atomic bombing of Japan
> The Potsdam and Yalta conferences
> Passage of the National Security Act
> The Marshall Plan
> The Truman Doctrine
> The Korean War
> Development of the hydrogen bomb
> The War in Indochina
> The coups or invasions in Guatemala, Brazil, Vietnam, Cyprus, Cuba, Lebanon, and Laos
> Berlin
> The Taft-Hartley Act
> The 1946 Full Employment Act
> The 1949 Public Housing Act

The several latter decisions, about public economic policy, obviously involved the participation of labor unions and liberal groups in public debate and conflict. But, Mills could point out, in the first place, these decisions were rather minor compared with those on procurement, reconversion, and the Marshall Plan; and, second, each of the decisions complied with the underlying points of consensus.

This strategy also permitted Mills to introduce the concept of conspiracy in a sophisticated and contexted way, rather than in the crude ways it is often applied. Having argued that a massive institutional machinery is at work, Mills can suggest that an "inner core" of men must be produced as a logical component of the system. The "inner core" is composed of men whose biographies consist of interchanging roles in political, military, and economic circles. Men of important legal and financial experience are a good but by no means only example, of the functionaries required by the interlocked structures of power.

Mills offered little documentation of this thesis, making only a cryptic comment about a few "key (law) firms." Again, other documentation of this "inner core" is sparse. Suzanne Keller, however, points out that at least some suggestive information has developed. Her own study of the American business elite of 1950 located a "core elite of British, old family, upper middle and middle class Protestant business leaders who were concentrated in the older established business fields of manufacturing, transportation and finance." The studies of Lloyd Warner and James Abegglen also found a core group "in the leaders of the more stable companies and among brokers, dealers, and investment bankers." These studies, however, are quite inconclusive because of the failure of the authors to really locate the elite, in terms of role and function, in the total social system. Needless to say, the empirical problems here are momentous, especially since there is no legal way of obtaining real information about the work of these core groups: the military is classified, and the business community is exempt because of its private status. Given these immense restrictions, Mills's theory rests on the only appeal that it finally can: that complementary institutions produce and need a circulating elite of power.

Mills was a dramatist of the times. Understanding this, it is explainable why, in a society that avoids the recognition of power, he employed colorful phraseology in his depiction of the power elite: corporation chieftains, professional warlords, political directors, and so on. This flair should not obscure the fact that Mills was employing a formal and rigorous sociological theory. Derived from Max Weber and stated most comprehensively in his work with H. H. Gerth, *Character and Social Structure* (1953), this theory supposed society as the interaction of separate institutional orders. Each of these orders, composed of the role activities of thousands of individuals, performs a necessary function in maintaining and changing the social order.

For Mills and Gerth, and Weber before them, *institutional orders* are all those institutions having similar consequences and ends or that serve similar objective functions. The articulated relationship of all the institutional orders is the *social structure*. The social structure of American society, like that of all societies, is composed of five orders:

- The *political* order consists of those institutions in which people acquire, wield, or influence the distribution of power and authority within social structures.
- The *economic* order is made up of those establishments by which people organize labor, resources, and technical implements in order to produce and distribute goods and services.
- The *military* order is composed of institutions in which people organize legitimate violence and supervise its use.
- The *kinship* order is made of institutions that regulate and facilitate legitimate sexual intercourse, procreation, and the early rearing of children.
- The *religious* order is composed of those institutions in which people organize and supervise the collective worship of God or deities, usually at regular intervals and at fixed places.

These orders do not always bear the same relation to each other. Shifts in the patterns of dominance signify the transition from one epoch to another. "The model of historical change characteristic of a given epoch will thus be more or less an inference from the types of interaction which prevail in the social structure we are examining."

Integration—Mills's alternative to orthodox elite theory—is measured by the kind and degree of *correspondence, coincidence, coordination,* and *convergence* of the major institutional orders.

- *Correspondence* is the unification of a social structure "by the working out in its several institutional orders of a common structural principle, which thus operates in a parallel way in each"—For instance, the classic free enterprise model in which persons demand freedom from dominance in their economic, political, marital, and other choices.
- *Coincidence* involves "different structural principles or developments in various orders [which] result in their combined effects in the same, often unforeseen, outcome of unity for the whole society." Here Mills gave as an example the decline

of feudal codes and the development of an administration and legal framework that facilitated the rise of capitalism. Agreeing with Weber's classic analysis, he pictured the two trends—normative code and economic organization—as causally anchored in two separate institutional orders.

- *Coordination* involves the "integration of society by means of one or more institutional orders which become ascendant over other orders and direct them; thus other orders are regulated or managed by the ascendant order or orders." Here the example is a "totalitarian" society, specifically Nazi Germany. Mills's explanation, drawn largely from Franz Neumann, was this: The German economic order centralized into a cartel situation while the political order fragmented into a variety of parties, each too weak to control the results of the economic concentration. Into this situation came a new party, as the representative of the new state, and the agency of coordination. The party exploits mass despair. It brings the political, military, and economic orders into close correspondence. It finds numerous points of coincidence and correspondence in the military and economic order. It forges a totalitarian state, frames the policy goals for all the institutional orders, and decimates independent points of power wherever they exist. (Without recognizing it, Mills at this point was echoing Marx's theory, expressed in *The Eighteenth Brumaire,* of the "Napoleonic state" that develops in periods of class deadlock; characteristically, Mills attributed his thinking in this matter to Weber.)
- *Convergence* involves "two or more institutional orders [which] coincide to the point of fusion; they become one institutional set up." As an instance of this, Mills suggested the frontier experience in which the farmer is also a soldier and his household a small military outpost.

How a society integrates, and what the weight and relationship between institutional orders are, are questions that Mills deliberately left open. Two alternative answers were rejected.

The first, the "monistic hunch," assumes one of the orders to be the engine of change in all the rest. The second, "principled pluralism," assumes there is no causal force visible. Mills's own prescription was to search for the causes of "specific historical sequences"—"those causes which according to experience and the conventional standards of scientific evidence satisfy our curiosity." Insisting on the need to find a "way in" to the many interconnected spheres that make up society, Mills and Gerth professed that the "easiest 'way in' involves examination of those institutional orders in which roles are implemented by control over things that require joint activities"—for example, the means of production, communication, war, administration, "in other words, the economic, the military and the political order." What is immediately relevant today, they claimed, are the new developments and complementary relationships in the economic and military orders.

The other major way of characterizing society that they employed was the system of *stratification,* which intersects the system of *institutional orders* in a variety of ways. Again with their main reliance on Max Weber, Mills and Gerth cited four important keys, or dimensions, of stratification: *occupation, class, status,* and *power.*

- *Occupation* is a set of activities "pursued more or less regularly as a major source of income."
- *Class* "in its simplest objective sense has to do with the amount and source (property or work) of income as these affect the chances of people to obtain other available values."
- *Status* "involves the successful realization of claims to prestige; it refers to the distribution of deference in a society."
- *Power* "refers to the realization of one's will, even if this involves the resistance of others."

The interrelation of these four dimensions is very complex, but one matter should be vividly pointed out. Mills seemed to assign equal relevance to each of them while implicitly his argument seemed to make class and occupation the greatest contributors to stratification. They both refer to the economic order, but "each may be deeply and intricately involved in the other orders." As for status, Mills said it is dependent on class as a "limiting or conditioning factor." As for power, at least insofar as determining state policy is concerned, it is used directly by or indirectly in the interests of those with the greatest advantages in the economic stratas. However, Mills did not draw these conclusions and observations into a general theory. Marxism remained a hint within a general Weberian framework.

The theoretical connection between the two classifications schemes—institutional orders and stratification factors—was summarized as follows:

> That institutional order which is dominant in a social structure (power) will usually be the order in which status is primarily anchored and upheld.... High class position and preferred occupations will also, given sufficient time, be acquired by those that are heads of the most powerful institutional order.

If the class situation "conditions and limits" the distribution of status (here one must recall Engels's equally peculiar observation that the relations of production determined cultural form and content only in an "ultimate" sense), and if the ruling institutional order is that order "in which status is primarily anchored and upheld," then why not call the ruling institutional order a ruling *class*? To be sure, there are occasions in which this pattern will be aborted. For instance, a military coup d'état might be accomplished by a group of mixed-class character, against the short- and long-term interests of the ruling class. However, as Mills admitted, if the ruling group is to be viable in its role, then it would soon acquire a "high class position and preferred occupation."

To move from Mills's stated position to the implied position would be to move very nearly from the Weberian to the Marxian perspective. It is certainly ludicrous to believe that Mills was in some secret way a Marxist draped with an orthodox Weberian mantle; it is ludicrous as well to think that Mills was unaware of the close similarity of his conclusions with Marxian ones. Perhaps the truth is that Weber and Marx contend directly in Mills's writings in a long and unresolved dialogue with each other. The continuity of this tension is obvious from a scanning of *Character and Social Structures* (1953), *The Power Elite* (1956), and *The Marxists* (1962).

In the first case, Mills and Gerth, like Weber, stressed the introduction of political institutions and rules into the twentieth-century economy, thus giving the political order "increasing weight and influence upon the economic bases of stratification." Does this mean the political order is *equally* endowed with "weight and influence"? Apparently not: "The 'welfare state' in the United States now attempts to relieve class tensions and build a mighty defense force without modifying basic class structure."

In *The Power elite,* Mills attributes causal abilities to each of the separate orders that comprise the power elite, and he explains the motion of the elite in terms of the changing relative strengths of the three orders. But he also writes that the Marxian doctrine of class struggle is "closer to reality than any assumed harmony of interests." And Mills's own empirical findings suggest that the most general identification of the elite is with the corporate property system.

In *The Marxists,* Mills was critical of Marxism for the single-factor analysis, but he also could write this:

Class struggle in the Marxist sense does not *prevail*; conflicts of economic interests have quite generally been institutionalized; they are subject to indirect and bureaucratic decision, rather than to open and political battle. There are, of course, basic class conflicts of interest. But—there is little struggle over them.

In *The Marxists* also he reformulated a position that was at least implicit in *The New Men of Power.* This is the concept of a "capitalist political economy" as an alternative to either the pure ruling class or institutional models. In this view he reinserted the enlarged political stratum into an economic framework: thus the motor of historical change was not so much the economic base but the *joined* political and economic institutions.

> This kind of political capitalism Marx neither knew nor foresaw. He did not grasp the almost neo-mercantilist form it has taken nor the extent and effects of politically controlled and subsidized capitalism. The subsidies have been direct and indirect, of a welfare and a military nature. That they may be considered subsidies of the economic defaults of capitalism does not alter my point: it strengthens it.

There is evidence, too, in *The Marxists,* that Mills felt himself in the Weberian and Marxian traditions simultaneously—but as their synthesizer, not as an ambiguous descendent. He said, for instance, that

> we must generalize Marx's approach to economics. We come to focus—as did Marx—upon the changing techniques of economic control. But we also focus—as did Max Weber—upon the techniques of military violence, of political struggle and administration, and upon the means of communication—in short, upon *all* the means of power, and upon their quite varied relations with one another in historically specific societies.

Whether these orders can be separated so easily, whether Marx and Weber ultimately are compatible theorists, is the question Mills did not answer. *The Power Elite* surely was more of an ambiguity than a synthesis.

In one of his numerous edifying footnotes, Mills said the power elite is a "status group"—that is, a repository of deference. Unfortunately, he did not clarify it explicitly, as a kind of social structure. In his terms, we might infer that it is an articulation of the economic, military, and, to a lesser extent, political orders, with the others more or less subordinate. (Which institutional order happens to be dominant was, for Mills, an empirically open question: his answer was the corporate and military orders.) The modes of integration of the power elite would include correspondence, coincidence, coordination, and convergence, all of them lacking full development, but all sufficiently existing to be described as a trend or a main thrust.

In still another footnote, he made a very important explanation of why he rejected the "ruling class" concept. He described it as a *short cut*, which did not leave sufficient autonomy to the political and military orders.

> It should be clear that we do not accept as adequate the simple view that high economic men unilaterally make all decisions of national consequence. We hold that such a simple view of "economic determinism" must be elaborated by "political determinism" and "'military determinism"; that the higher agents of these three domains now often have a noticeable degree of autonomy; and that only in the often intricate ways of coalition do they make up and carry through the most important decisions.

Mills seemed quite correct in trying to develop an elaborate theory of the mechanics of change, more elaborate at least than one in which specifically economic men control decisions in all spheres. And he was justified, undoubtedly, in criticizing Marxist or ruling class theories where they employed shortcut devices. But he was dismissing not economic determinism but a specific, oversimplified, and mechanical variant of it.

The major question might be formulated this way: Is the social structure an articulation of the related institutional orders, or rather, are institutional orders the functionally divided expressions of more basically stratified social structure? This is the kind of question raised by Robert S. Lynd in his papers on power and in his reviews of Mills's books. Lynd defines social structure in terms of the organized stratification system. It is, for him,

> the organized relations of groups and categories of people identified within a given society according to kinship, sex, age, division

of labor, race, religion, or another criteria stressed as differentiating people in role, status, access to resources, and authority. This structure establishes durable relations that hold groups of people together for certain purposes and separates them for others. Such a social structure may persist over many generations. Its continuance depends upon its ability to cope with historical changes that involve absorption of new groupings and relations of men without fundamental change in the structure of the society of a kind that involves major transfer of power.

If the social structure is founded in arbitrary or imposed inequalities in the distribution of life chances, then the institutional system will be one of organized inequality in the distribution of power. From this point of view, in which power is generated by the social structure through the institutions, business and government have the same structural basis, and exchanges between them are, in Lynd's metaphor, merely the transfer of articles from one pocket to another on a single pair of trousers. An oversimplified, but basically exact, explanation of the political economy thus could be constructed as an alternative to the Weber-Mills explanation. It would be that the nineteenth- and early twentieth-century social structure, expressed through market institutions and later through the large corporation, worked to the benefit of those who immediately controlled the productive system. At a certain point in the industrialization process, instability occurred in the social structure from two directions. First, capitalist production tended to saturate markets, leading to overproduction and declining profit. Second, the threat of an antagonized labor force required stabilization of the business cycle. The political institutions of subsidized welfare capitalism thus developed.

This continuity of social structure, reflected in the institutions of society, seems a more valid approach than Mills's view of separate institutional orders together articulating the social structure. This largely is because it permits a less mysterious manner of explaining an identity of interests among the separate orders. In Mills's conceptual framework, correspondence, coincidence, and convergence *happen* without human intention. An identity of interests among institutions comes about, not because some of them exist to defend or ratify the economic order, but because complementary activity goes on in a *parallel* way. This is possible theoretically if it is admitted that the institutions truly are separate, discrete units. But Mills himself did not seem to believe they were, except for purposes of conceptual clarity. In reality, then, people simultaneously act out a number of roles: as producers, consumers, employees, voters, worshippers, parents, and so forth. What conditions the content of these roles if it is not the economic situation? True, many people "betray" their class interest by identifying with the interests of others. But "class" does not mechanically determine a person's action; it rather suggests the limits within which the aggregate of persons, living in similar conditions, will live and die. The particular life and death of individuals are shaped by the specific experiences, many of which are uniquely theirs and which, cumulatively, can push them to activity outside their class norms. This kind of individual behavior, however, by no means denies the fact that certain people are advantaged, and others disadvantaged, by their role in the productive system. Nor does it deny that these roles, in a broad and rough way, allocate the possibilities for education, medical treatment, mobility, and other valued resources moreso than any other roles.

Engels at one point mentioned that he and Marx never elaborated sufficiently the role of the "superstructure," and, therefore, it became simply a "reflex" of the "material base." In any *stable* society, the government, within the Marx-Engels perspective, is the "executive committee of the ruling class." The failure of Marx and Engels to concentrate on elaborating this thesis (for instance, what kind of "determining power" did the government have?) set the conditions for wholesale oversimplifications in later Marxian theory. Lynd does not rectify the unfortunate results of this trend but reinforces them by making the institutional order analogous to the pocket on a pair of trousers. Where Mills is quite sound is in his opposition to the "shortcut" and in his insistence that modern elites have "considerable autonomy" due to the institutional resources available to them and their broad area of discretionary power to take legitimate action. For instance, the Joint Chiefs of Staff or the Strategic Air Command are able to overturn governments, cause border flare-ups, initiate preventive war, or seize the government of the United States—against the wishes of corporation leaders. Less dramatically the president is able to make military and economic decisions daily that affect market opportunities, employment levels, investment schedules, and world alliances. The "ruling class," moreover, is muddled as to its own interests. And this, along with the bureaucratic obstacle course inherent in a massively institutional society, prevents any *direct* control of the political and military establishments by the economic order. (Lest this theory be taken too literally, it should be noted that the present secretaries of defense, state, and commerce still are among the most important corporate leaders of the last three decades.)

Mills has to be honored for avoiding the shortcut. At the same time, his own empirical studies of the tripartite elite suggested an immense continuity of interest among all groups in preserving the corporation property system more than any other social value. Is it not the most unquestioned sector of the status quo? Does not an examination of the political "outsiders," the congressional politicians and the military leaders again and again lead back to the dominant role of the institutions and values of corporation capitalism?

Mills occasionally inveighed against this interpretation, as when he said it would be

> quite mistaken to believe that the political apparatus is merely an extension of the corporate world, or that it has been taken over by the representatives of the corporate rich. The American government is not in any simple way nor as a structural fact, a "committee of the ruling class." This is a network of "committees" and other men from other hierarchies besides the corporate rich sit upon these committees.

But a dominant theme, certainly, was that the political order stabilized and subsidized capitalism. This cannot be explained in terms of correspondence or coincidence alone; it can only be explained in terms of political "outsiders" and conscious interlocking as well:

> The propertied class, in an age of corporate property, has become a corporate rich, and in becoming corporate, has consolidated its power and drawn to its defense new men of more executive and more political stance.... Today the successful economic man ... must influence or control those positions in the state in which decisions of consequence to his corporate activities are made. This trend is facilitated by the war, which thus creates the need to continue corporate activities with political as well as economic means.... During war the political economy tends to become more unified and, moreover, political legitimations of the most unquestionable sort—national security itself—are gained for corporate economic activities.

But to establish that the corporation is political and general in its effect and its toll is insufficient. Mills's material on the political order suggested that its function is to support the prevailing economic order, He mainly concentrated on the executive branch ("the political directorate"), and there he found that fully two-thirds of the executive staff were men who gained their career experience in business and, less frequently, in military endeavors. These were the political "outsiders," and, as such, they were bred to see public government as an ally of private business.

Mills also considered Congress, but too much in terms of its structured inability to cope extensively with international affairs. Had he paid more attention to its composition, however, he would have found evidence for the thesis that institutional elites express the tensions inherent in a social structure. Congress, especially at that time, was composed primarily of rural, southern, and politically conservative forces, deriving their security from a seniority system in Congress and gerrymandered safe districts at home. Given this base of representation, Congress functions as a lingering outlet for the recalcitrant small businessmen and independent producers. It reflects the traditional private enterprise elements of a social structure in which privately planned corporations have transformed the market system in their rise to dominance. This has created a contradiction between Congress and the new political "outsiders" and their corporate allies. In his 1959 study of one hundred senators and the one hundred largest corporation presidents, Andrew Hacker delineated these differences quite clearly. Differences between the two elites existed (1) in the site of hometowns, with the greater number of corporate leaders coming from urban centers; (2) in the character of education, with businessmen tending to an Ivy League past as opposed to the usual state university experiences of the senators; (3) in their current religious affiliation, with nearly all businessmen connected to the high-status Protestant denominations, and senators tending to be affiliated with the church of highest status in their locale; (4) in education of children, with most businessmen planning a private or Ivy League education for their young, while the senators expected state-supported education for theirs; (5) in career mobility, with the executives less rooted in specific locales than the senators.

Hacker concluded:

> At the heart of the executive plaint is the feeling that our legislators cannot bring themselves to acknowledge that corporations are here to stay and national in character. It is wrong, they would argue, to treat a major corporation as simply another "pressure group" bent on getting a larger share of the spoils.... [On the one hand,] there is, in the corporate world, no small anxiety about the politics of democracy, as they are expressed in legislation. This is not because the politics are democratic but rather because they are focused through a provincial lens rather than a metropolitan one.... [On the other hand,] the legislators are faced with a power they do not really understand and with demands about whose legitimacy they are uneasy. If they acquiesce, it is with no small qualm of conscience. At the same time, they are unable to protect the small local enterprises to which they are ideologi-

cally committed. Small business loans and anti-trust legislation are ineffective instruments, yet these are the major weapons in a paper arsenal.

From such a contradiction there can come a deadlock, if the contending forces are equally powerful—but, as Hacker notes, the small business system, and therefore Congress, has been marginal and weakening.

In summary, the political directorate of "outsiders" was composed of corporate and military personnel, and Congress operated at the "middle levels," not because of its unsuitable structure for foreign policy primarily, but because of its character as a remnant of the older market system.

The military also can be explained as a special segment of one class but, unlike Congress, a segment that was ascendant during the 1940s and 1950s.

In *The New Men of Power,* Mills demonstrated an awareness of the fast rise of the military into policymaking circles due to strategic needs that otherwise could not be met. He suggested also the complementary relationships, and increasing fusion, of military and industrial men. He went further to point out that the military was emerging into an officially political role, perhaps most notably in the case of General George C. Marshall who served as secretary of state (1947–1949) and as a main architect of American foreign strategy. He feared that these trends would accelerate so long as a "military definition of reality" prevailed among so-called civilian policymakers.

An understanding of the pace of the military ascendance from 1940 and its exact character are important background to an appraisal of the power elite concept. Although Mills never stressed it thematically, his material on the military, as published from 1948 to 1956, supports the judgment that the military were involved nearly everywhere in U.S. policymaking, but as a group subordinate to the economic elite and the "political outsiders" (one of whom was the president of the United States). The contention here is that not only was the military "directly" subordinate (controllable by the executive) but that it was "indirectly" subordinate to class interest. Mills's thesis of the military as an elite with powers of independent action (the conception fully elaborated in *The Power Elite*) neglected the origins and identity of the military within the political economy of capitalism in the 1940s.

The last years of the New Deal did involve a public policy stress on the welfare of the working classes, and from the Temporary National Economic Committee a questioning of monopoly concentration, but it did not alter the basic relations of private property. By 1938, the reform tide was smothered in a tremendous conservative reaction from Congress and corporations. The possibility of domestic social change was checked, and under increasing trade competition from Japan, Germany, and Italy, Roosevelt and other New Dealers were debating by the late 1930s whether or not to go to war. William Appleman Williams notes that Allen Dulles, of Sullivan and Cromwell (the law firm Mills and others describe as being at the "core" of the power elite) and later the director of the Central Intelligence Agency, "advised corporation leaders in 1937 to 'dismiss the idea' that any neutrality legislation would 'have any ... influence in keeping us out of war.'" In a war substantially fought over America's market relationships with Germany, Japan, and Italy, a war that effectively would abolish unemployment and underproduction, it was natural and necessary that business and political leaders would come together in policy-making roles more extensively, cooperatively, and interchangeably than at any previous time in the century. Over the years 1940–1944, two-thirds of all prime supply contracts went to America's one hundred largest corporations—and almost one-third went to the largest ten corporations. The largest 250 corporations, which owned 65 percent of all facilities in 1939, came to operate 80 percent of all new privately operated facilities built with government funds during the war, and they held nearly 80 percent of all active prime war supply contracts in September 1944.

There probably is no way to characterize the outlook of the big industrialists toward the new military caste. But the famous letters by Lammot du Pont and Alfred Sloan about General Motors board policies in 1945 may be suggestive of an air of friendly superiority. Du Pont was replying to the proposal that General Marshall be seated among the corporate rich in the GM board room. He wrote, "My reasons for not favoring his membership on the board are: First, his age; second, his lack of stockholdings; and third, his lack of experience in industrial business affairs." Sloan observed, "General Marshall might do us some good when he retires, following his present assignment—assuming he continues to live in Washington; recognizing the position he holds in the community and among the government people and the acquaintances he has—and if he became familiar with our thinking."

In short, circles of men at the very centers of financial and industrial power fought against the welfare and reform thrust of the New Deal; they entered the political establishment as its indispensable producers during the war years; they saw to it that the postwar framework of policy would seek trade expansion and full domestic employment without changes in the private elite character of control over investment; they profited by interaction with the new, rising military bureaucracy.

The new military establishment also was dependent on the economic elite for its expansion and legitimacy in the 1940s. This is not to say that the generals and admirals were impotent subordinates of the national business and political leadership. Obviously the military were among the most competent, aggressive, and instrumental groups involved in the war. However, Mills's own evidence points to a timidity, or status anxiety, among members of the traditional military that tended to mitigate their ability to adroitly take advantage of new chances for power. More important, it was the business and political community that initiated the "opening" for the military that permitted the rise of military men to policy command posts and the postwar conscription of the military into key industrial slots. The more aggressive "militarists" often were the businessmen themselves who were called to Washington to take over the new defense establishment.

Not until 1947, with passage of the National Security Act, was there a military *institutionalization* sufficient to create a functioning professional elite. The act set up the major agencies that compose the military hierarchy to this day: a separate air force equal to the army and navy, the Joint Chiefs of Staff, National Security Council, Central Intelligence Agency, and the largest single organization in the world, the Department of Defense itself.

To understand the process of military development, it is instructive to follow the career progression of James Forrestal, the first secretary of defense. Forrestal was the president of Dillon, Read in the late 1930s and an implacable anticommunist whose military views could be summarized in his businesslike remark "There are no returns on appeasement." He came to Washington during the war at the call of the president; there he became undersecretary of the navy and, later, full secretary. In that capacity he organized the National Security Industrial Association, an avowedly long-term apparatus of the military-industrial complex, before the beginning of official American-Soviet bitterness in 1945. As secretary of defense in 1948, he appeared before the first graduating class of the Armed Forces Information School and encouraged the growth of aggrandizing and propaganda mechanisms within the military establishment. He told his audience, "Part of your task is to make people realize that the Army, Navy and Air Force are not external creations but come from and are part of the people. It is your responsibility to make citizens aware of their responsibilities to the services."

Forrestal's public relations staffs, different budgets, a variety of military strategies, subsidized research, development, and testing soon appeared as signs of the military's *internal* dynamic. The achievement of Universal Military Training, the first peacetime selective service, was an early test and victory for the military. Finally, there came the war-preparedness buildup, which culminated in the Korean War. In those years there matured an elite capable of producing a defense machine second to none, as well as a general who would "end the war" as president.

But it would be lopsided to insist with Mills on the *independence* of the military elite from the political economy. More reasonably, it is visible as an elite with "autonomy" *within* the broad purposes of the political economy. It is possible for such an elite to act *aberrantly*; for example, a preventive war started by a clique of generals is very possible, contrary to the wishes of many corporate leaders. But the abnormality of such an event suggests further the point that the normal function of the military elite is to defend the political economy. Abnormal, unexpected events illustrate that social controls are not perfect. But they do not show that the military elite is free of the social controls that direct it to serve the social structure. It is also possible to view the military as having a certain kind of "determining" power on the social structure—for example, when the air force succeeds in receiving an appropriation for a bomber despite the intentions of political and economic elites. But this is not sufficient to prove the fundamental independence of an elite from the originating causal relationship imposed by the political economy itself. For instance, it is perfectly possible that the military-industrial complex (the defense contractors, services, lobbies, and politicians) could be diminished or dismantled altogether without a change in basic social structure.

Mills in later times pictured the growth in status of the military men as the attempt "to increase their powers and hence their status in comparison with politicians and business men." But this observation, however descriptive of a power drive, overlooked the basic reason for the military's existence: defense of the interests of the elite that sanctioned the military, which meant ultimately the defense of existing property relations. The burden of this historical interpretation, in short, is to insist on the property basis of postwar developments in the military establishment, and to suggest, further, the tendency for a new bureaucratic elite to develop needs and drives of its own once it is established. This does not answer the question of whether the military is an autonomous causal force in the history, which Mills raised in his "departure" from Marxism. It redefines the problem, however, pointing to the economic and political roots of the military that shape its purpose and suggests that, to the extent a built-in aggrandizement drive occurs within the military, such a drive makes the organization tend toward a growing capability for initiative without veering it from the economic and political purposes in which it was originated. Perhaps the military indeed has autonomous causal power, but within a framework of value determined in the institutions of the political economy.

In another sense, however, it was a theoretical advance: Mills's work was a brilliant effort to elaborate what Marxism knew as the "superstructure." He once pointed out that, for Marxism, superstructure had become a residual category, something "into which to dump everything that is left over." It was Mills's important contribution, and one reflective of the unusual developments of the postwar period, to have seen the relevance of the new institutional agencies of power: "The institutional organization of society, including relations of production, certainly penetrated deeply into technological implements and their scientific developings, including forces of production, shaping their meaning and role in historical change."

Important as this insight was, however, it does not explain why Mills's three elites share so much in the way of social and class origins and general outlook. If one begins with the relative unanimity of the elites, granting to each a domain of autonomy with unknown, because *untested,* limits, then a different conception than Mills's takes shape. This alternative conception begins with a social structure favorable to those who control the production and distribution of valued resources. Through this position they are permitted the greatest share of material benefits; they control the investment of the fabulous resources of an integrated corporate economy; they create a general structure of opportunity for the whole society; they create an economic surplus that can be used to guarantee whatever influence can be purchased; they enjoy an opportunity to shape a political and legal structure to suit their social and economic needs. They are by no means unified internally. Indeed, contemporary capitalism still lacks a theorist to make sense out of the muddle of financial and legal institutions, self-financing corporations, state-subsidized activity, and independent market players.

Moreover, the links of this body of economic men to the formal political spheres remains cloudy, although it is very clear that the relation is tense. That this is so today is reflected in the obvious tendency to enlarge the executive branch with corporate statesmen to compensate for the historic "lag" that anchors Congress to the market tradition.

Finally, the link to the military establishment is equally tense if only because of the unusually rapid rise of the "warlords" to a new world situation defined as requiring their unique skills. Indeed, the whole social structure contains antagonisms deeper than these, due particularly to the basing of privilege on (1) the arbitrary denial of opportunities to men sharing other class and racial situations and (2) the need for continuously expanding markets. The maintenance of a stable system of elite rule rests on the ability of the elite to satisfy, either materially or psychologically, or to forcefully suppress, those with relatively less influence over the decision-making apparatus of society.

This privileged elite can be called a "class," if that term is carefully defined. In the most common meaning, and that assigned by Weber and Mills, class is an economic category having to do with the distribution of valued resources through the market mechanism. But in a society where corporate forms are outmoding the market mechanism, class no longer can be defined in terms of the immediate ownership of property. It must signify at least a complex of owners and managers who *control* the economy. This class does not rule in any direct manner, although in the political order there can be found numerous individuals of this class position. In the transition from market to corporate economy, the perfection of social controls requires a political organization to such a degree that it is more valid to speak of a political economy than an economy. The "power elite," in short, is too diffuse a description of the basis of minority rule. "Corporate state," though imperfect in some respects also, is more accurate because of its focus on the joined political and economic institutions.

This statement is not a mere technical rearrangement of Mills's framework. It implies an inherent *instability* in capitalist political economy, due to the long-term needs to (1) maintain arbitrary class domination and (2) constantly create or expand markets for distribution and (3) control technological power for private ends. Mills, in *The Power Elite* and *The Marxists,* came to conclude that the main drift toward stability, foreseen in 1948, was likely to continue. What must be asked now is whether this stability was based on a long-term transcendence of capitalist instability or on a fantastic postwar abnormality. If the latter is the case, as our examination of the postwar boom tends to indicate, then it can be said that capitalist instabilities have been submerged in postwar "prosperity." This submerging would explain the seemingly independent force of military and political institutions. Were this the case, then conversely it would reduce the significance of institutions as units of social organization. It is paradoxical that Max Weber himself, the father of modern social equilibrium theory, came to the same (rarely noticed) judgment in his famous "Class, Status, Party":

> *Every technological repercussion and economic transformation threatens stratification by status and pushes the class situation to the foreground.* Epochs and countries in which the naked class situation is of predominant significance are regularly the periods of technological and economic transformation. And every slowing down of the shifting of economic stratifications leads, in due course, to the growth of status structures and makes for a resuscitation of the important role of social honor.

This view implies that there are disadvantaged classes whose freedom and opportunity at some point demand a change not merely in institutional but in basic social structure. Mills would not deny their existence but clearly leaned instead toward a differentiation of society in terms of the power elite and the mass society, an interpretation congruent with his thesis of stability. In doing this, Mills unintentionally fell into the classic power-negativism syndrome, since power is defined as domination. From here he went on to suggest that the power elite had virtually expropriated the possibility of popular sovereignty altogether. Always acknowledging the existence of class conflicts of interest, he was able to argue they were muted by the process of stabilization. The society of elites and masses was superimposed on the society of classes. To Mills, the superimposition was permanent, complete. But was this judgment premature?

Masses, Classes, and Agencies of Change

By the 1950s, Mills had become disillusioned with the idea of the working class as a viable agency of social change. In place of a society stratified most saliently in class terms, he described a society in which the rise of the power elite "rests upon, and in some ways is part of, the transformation of the publics of America into a mass society." To counter the militarist and manipulative inclinations of the power elite, if not actually to make social change, Mills called for the development of a morally enraged and politically responsible intellectual elite.

But were these valid conclusions about the fate of the "masses"? Or was Mills's conclusion premature and overdrawn? If there is reason to suspect so, then should we restore the working classes to a more fundamental role in the concept of change?

The Mass Society

In Mills's usage, "mass society" referred to a general situation enclosing specific strata, in particular the new middle and the working classes. First becoming a theme in his studies of the Puerto Ricans of New York, it was developed further in *White Collar* (1953), *The Power Elite* (1956), *The Causes of World War Three* (1958), and *The Marxists* (1962). It has seemed to many that Mills, with these concepts if not with the concept of the power elite itself, was merging for once with the orthodox social science dismissal of the traditional class analysis and class politics. Riesman, Kuznets, Lilienthal, and Berle were among the many laureates of an "income revolution" that had quietly transformed the United States into a satisfied, predominantly middle-class society. Some Americans, including government spokespeople, just now are becoming aware that this prognosis was an overoptimistic one, based on the false equation of the 1945–1950 trend with the future growth of the national economy. It is important to distinguish Mills from these chroniclers of affluence. While it is true that he did not emphasize poverty in his writings—although he acknowledged its existence in nearly every book—this neglect stemmed more from his pessimism about the potential power of the poor than from a real infatuation with the new ideologies of abundance.

It is equally vital to distinguish Mills partly from other critics of "mass society." This criticism became especially current in the United States in the Fascist and Stalinist periods (though it went back to de Tocqueville and earlier commentators as well), when a series of writers, notably Lederer, Ortega, and Fromm, discerned the emergence of a generation of "mass men," with broken primary and secondary ties, susceptible to the demagogic appeals of totalitarian leaders. This view maintained its fashion and, in one form or another, was indisputably one of the major themes of social and political commentary in the two decades during which Mills wrote. While most intellectuals deplored the emergent mass society from an aristocratic standpoint (Ortega, Marcel) or from a fear of its incipient totalitarianism (Arendt, Kornhauser, Mannheim), some saw in it a real democratic potential based on the right to privacy, free choice of friends and occupation, pluralistic norms, and the use of merit as an achievement criteria. Bell, Lipset, Gussman, and others generally have ratified in a positive way the arrival of the mass society.

Mills shared with these intellectuals a conceptual framework but little more. However, the conceptual framework itself was severely restricting. Foreshadowed in *Puerto Rican Journey* though expressed most systematically in *White Collar* and *The Power Elite,* Mills's mass society theory can be divided into theories of *structure, forms of control,* and *lifestyles.* He usually was sure to point out the strains in the massification system that pointed toward its rejection by aware citizens, but he nearly always doubted the prospect for this rejection. The distinguishing point, however, is that he discarded the possibility of fascism in the mass society that was stressed by many theorists, without adopting the celebrationist tone of the others. This was largely because Mills conceptually placed the mass society at the bottom of the social structure under the "middle levels of power" and the "power elite," while other theories viewed the tendency of mass behavior to become a subversive threat to a basically sound, pluralistic society. (For example, according to William Kornhauser, "the nihilism of the masses seems to be a greater threat to liberal democracy than the antagonisms between the classes.") With these differences held in mind, Mills's view of the mass society then can be expounded.

The organization of mass life, for Mills, revolved around a distinction between "structure" and "milieu." In the liberal classical theory, he said, the role of citizenship was supposedly such that the individual held a vantage point in the social system where he would give and take information, observe and analyze trends, and critically evaluate his interests in relation to public policy and national direction. The social prerequisites for this have been undercut severely, he said: communication flow is anonymous, impersonal, commercialized, organized, and manipulated by cliques in the mass media and political parties. The web of voluntary organizations is being integrated into the needs of the power elite and therefore transformed into a structure that ratifies already-made decisions or distracts the individual from his own real needs. Instead of a structural vantage point, the individual is isolated in a small immediate milieu that leaves him disconnected and powerless, though vaguely satisfied. Here he is prey to manipulation—that is, an impersonal and anonymous system of control offering no targets or enemies. In the absence of a way to crystallize personal troubles and find a genuine resolution, the people of mass society more and more are characterized by a personal anxiety and a political indifference. These were the master concepts for Mills, defining for him to a considerable extent the difference in public mood between the 1930s and the 1950s—the shift from issues orientation to mass anxiety.

As at other times, Mills mixed Marxian and Weberian concepts in his analysis. With Weber, he stressed the powerlessness imposed on the individual by the development of mass or bureaucratic organization; this often was done in Mills's finest lyrical form:

> [Man in mass society] takes things for granted, he makes the best of them, he tries to look ahead—a year or two perhaps, or even longer if he has children or a mortgage—but he does not seriously ask, What do I want? How can I get it? A vague optimism suffuses and sustains him, broken occasionally by little miseries and disappointments that are soon buried.... He loses his independence, and more importantly, he loses the desire to be independent: in fact, he does not have hold of the idea of being an independent individual with his own mind and his own-worked-out-way of life. It is not that he likes or does not like his life; it is that the question does not come up sharp and clear, so he is not bitter and he is not sweet about conditions and events. He thinks he wants merely to get his share of what is around with as little trouble as he can and with as much fun as possible.... Such order and movement as his life possesses is in conformity with external routines; otherwise his day-to-day experience is a vague chaos ... although he often does not know it because, strictly speaking, he does not truly possess or observe his own experience. He does not formulate his desires; they are insinuated into him. And, in the mass, he loses the self-confidence of the human being—if indeed he ever had it. For life in a society of masses implants insecurity and furthers impotence; it makes men uneasy and vaguely anxious; it isolates the individual from the solid group; it destroys firm group standards. Acting without standards the man in the mass just feels pointless.

The Marxism framework also was apparent, however, in his avoidance of blaming bureaucracy per se as the controlling and castrating force. Indeed, he often linked the absence of a "true" bureaucracy in Weber's sense, a rational administrative unit, with the inability of masses to become aroused by public issues—bureaucracy for Mills remained a device of the power elite used deliberately (and even indeliberately) to conceal elite activity and blur the senses of the masses. From this framework that permitted the imputing of blame, Mills was able to look pessimistically for the sources of protest. From *The New Men of Power* to *The Marxists,* Mills saw capitalist stability based on the long-term capacity to produce material satisfaction, institutionalize conflict, and distort mass consciousness through the communications media. These were the essential forces causing political acquiescence or apathy. However, in a dialectical sense, Mills was aware that capitalism's tendencies toward overproduction provided the potential basis for mass dissatisfaction: the traditional frontier opportunities of America were declining; the media were reinforcing an unfocused anxiety. For Mills the need to mobilize "mass man" was as vital as the need for constraint seen by pluralist theories of mass society mobilization into *publics* where reason and freedom would replace anxiety and political idiocy.

This mobilization would not occur magically, he knew, but only through the combination of a social crisis and effective radical leadership. His tendency, after 1948, was always to judge that crises could be managed by the welfare-capitalist system, though the seeds of renewed class conflict were always present. ("There are, of course, basic class conflicts. But there is little class struggle over them.") He emphatically denounced the default of leadership. He broadened his 1948 attack on labor leaders to the "cultural apparatus" in the 1950s—the intellectuals, writers, artists, churchmen, and professionals who complied with the cold war consensus.

Scientists become subordinated parts of the Science Machines of overdeveloped nations; these machines have become essential parts of the apparatus of war; that apparatus is now among the prime causes of war; without scientists it could not be developed and maintained. Thus do scientists become helpful and indispensable technicians of the thrust toward war.

Preachers, rabbis, priests—standing in the religious default—allow immorality to find support in religion; they use religion to cloak and to support impersonal, wholesale murder and the preparation for it. They condone the intent to murder millions of people by clean-cut young men flying and aiming intricate machineries toward Euro-Asia....

Intellectuals accept without scrutiny official definitions of world reality. Some of the best of them allow themselves to be trapped by the politics of anti-Stalinism, which has been a main passageway from the political thirties to the intellectual fault of the political fifties. They live and work in a benumbing society without living and working in protest and in tension with its moral and cultural insensibilities. They use the liberal rhetoric to cover the conservative default. They do not make available the knowledge and the sensibility required by publics, if publics are to hold responsible those who make decisions and in the name of the nation. They do not set forth reasons for human anger and give to it suitable targets.

What Mills once called the "occupational salad"—the new middle classes— figured prominently in his view of mass society, for mass society was a "multiclassed" society divided mainly into underdogs, the working class, and the new stratum of salaried employees. Though not always clear, Mills tended to place the new middle class closer to the working class than to the power elite, although their aspirations as white-collar salaried personnel were pointed upward to the higher circles.

Objectively ... the structural position of the white collar mass is becoming more and more similar to that of the wage-workers. Both are, of course, propertyless and their incomes draw closer and closer together. All the factors of their status position, which have enabled white collar workers to set themselves apart from wage-workers, are now subject to definite decline.

In terms of property, white collar people are *not* "in between capital and labor." They are in exactly the same property-class position as the wage-workers. They have no direct financial tie to the means of production, no prime claim on the proceeds from property.

This trend certainly has continued, reaching perhaps a qualitatively new stage with the automation since 1960 of many white-collar jobs; the *Wall Street Journal* has reported widespread consensus that the numbers of the employed white-collar personnel in banks, insurance companies, and similar institutions is leveling after its fifteen-year expansion.

But Mills was quite pessimistic about the chance for autonomous political organization of the white-collar (constituency). This class is defined by its very lack of consciousness; it is without "common symbols of loyalty, demand or hope"; it is fragmented into multiple occupational and status spheres—therefore, it is profoundly detached from politics. It was here that Mills employed the term *idiots,* borrowing from Aristotle, which has led many critics to suspect him of elitism. But in this context Mills could hardly be called elitist for searching out new agencies of change and ultimately clinging to the view that Western intellectuals are at least capable of a defensive holding action in behalf of reason and freedom. He did not "abandon" the lower classes as much as he abandoned a dogmatic expectation of their radicalization. This was clear, for example, from the probing way he considered the new middle class. "The white collar workers can only derive their strength from 'business' or from 'labor.' In the whole structure of power they are dependent variables." Given this, he expected they would be "rearguarders," following the drift of power. To be sure, there was some hope in the concept of white-collar unionism, especially where these people received a personal exposure to the "dramatic force" of unions, Mills thought. In all likelihood, however, this would not occur, *but not because of the "idiocy" of the white-collar masses so much as the default of the trade unions and cultural workmen.* This is a rather important point because it indicates the unique conception Mills had of the relation of the power elite to mass society. Mills's theory stressed the manipulative, counterinsurgent, and integrative resources of the elite, not the "nihilism" or inferiority of the masses. Here his analyses of the working and middle classes join: both classes share a modest sort of material satisfaction; they are submerged in milieu to be battered by the obfuscating imagery of the media; they lack effective radical leadership. That the one remains a class and the other an occupational scatter is temporary: the income and prestige levels of the groups are equalizing, and together they are forming a mass society that decomposes the class structure. They have no responsible leaders.

It is difficult to deal critically with Mills's argument because much of it is based on "latent data." For instance, it is impossible to measure the extent of elite "resources" because the elites *have not been profoundly challenged.* Likewise, it is impossible to gauge the effect that "radical leadership" might have on popular consciousness because such leadership has not appeared. There is, however, some evidence to support the proposition that union and political leaders do not tap potential sources of radical or militant involvement among the rank and file. What is especially interesting about this evidence is that it was accumulated, though not all reported, during the early 1950s when it was highly fashionable to blame the constituent rather than the leadership stratum for the failure of liberal and radical movements. Lipset's *Political Man* and *Union Democracy,* while containing much argument contrary to Mills's, also pointed out the variety of ways in which unions co-opt new leaders from the rank and file: "Aspiring members are, however, usually subjected to a barrage of administrative views on economics, politics, and union organization. Mobility within the union structure requires that the aspirant take over the norms and orientations dominant in the organization—that is, those held by the leaders."

Perhaps the most important study recently in this field is Sidney Peck's participant observation in various Milwaukee unions in the early 1950s. Arguing against the orthodox thesis that workers are just occupation and wage oriented rather than class oriented, Peck found widespread class consciousness (defined as a "mentality which identifies one's socio-economic predicament with untold others who are considered to be similarly situated"). Peck's conclusion was that "political 'apathy,' when it results from the lack of a meaningful political choice, may be the *considered class response* of workers who believe they are being misled."

Recent other studies, notably those by Leggett, find that "uprootedness" and union affiliations tend to create a class consciousness among workers. Manis and Meltzer, studying textile workers in the early 1950s, found that job- rather than class-consciousness was created because the union accepted the given order and concentrated only on better wage bargaining.

One of the most amazing examples of a latent radicalism can be found in the statistical information on Detroit autoworkers compiled by Kornhauser, Sheppard, and Mayer during the same period. This was a major study done for the United Auto Workers; and, first of all, its explicit conclusions were noteworthy:

> [Worker's feelings] remain formless and unspecified except as they are given meaning and direction by the opinion-molding influences of the society…. If they go conservative, it will not be because economic prosperity compels it but because liberal leadership—including prominently liberal leadership in organized labor—fails to reach them with convincing alternative social-political interpretations that fit their own fundamental needs.

However, an examination of the sample taken for the study reveals even more relevant information. The authors divide the sample into several categories, two of which are "Prolabor Political" and "Prolabor Apolitical"—groups sympathetic with the work of the union but differentiated by their level of actual political interest and involvement (see table 2.6).

The statistics show an underdog class, three-fourths white but including more Negroes than among the "politicals"; poorly educated; predominantly low-skilled; exploited at less than

Table 2.6 Prolabor Political and Apolitical Groups

	Prolabor Political (%)	Prolabor Apolitical (%)
Race		
White	98	76
Negro	2	24
Education		
8 years or less	14	80
9 years or less	86	20
Occupation		
Skilled	54	7
Semiskilled	46	93
Individual income		
Under $3,000	———	37
$3,000–$3,999	23	44
$4,000–$4,999	27	13
Years in Detroit		
23 or more	45	44
All of life	8	37

Source: Adapted from Kornhauser, Mayer, and Sheppard, Labor Votes.

minimum wages; residents of long standing in the community. They have the orientation but not the motivation. They have seen leaders come and go, undoubtedly, and issues, too; they are not going all-out for district reapportionment and other issues the union makes its focus. But the Negroes at least are undoubtedly a group "reached" in the 1960s by the northern civil rights movement; the whites have not been reached, but who has tried?

Data such as these suggest the need for a reinterpretation of the thesis of "working-class authoritarianism" that became so fashionable, for instance, in the early 1950's work of Lipset and Stouffer. Both of these analysts used essentially middle-class criteria to conclude that people are fundamentally antidemocratic. Lipset, in his reviews of various survey findings, and Stouffer, in his studies of responses to civil liberties problems, were concerned basically with the norm of tolerance as a criteria of true democratic beliefs and behavior. Both found, of course, that more complex and tolerant views were characteristic of the middle-class persons interviewed. However, it was implicitly assumed that the tolerance was a real *ethic*; another interpretation, that "tolerance" in the sense used is little more than a class response to the fact of being socially integrated and security oriented, was neither considered nor refuted. The critical difference, in other words, might not be between middle-class "tolerance" and working-class "extremism," but between degrees of vested interest in prevailing economic and political relations.

None of this assumes a latent rebellious sentiment in the lower classes. Indeed, it is difficult to dispute the summary findings of Robert E. Lane, that "a labor market which provides fluid channels for men of ability to rise in the occupational scale discourages the search for political means of expression.... These features of the labor market deprive society of certain sources of political bitterness and so contribute to the emotionally low-pitched 'politics of happiness.'"

The evidence obviously supports Mills's finding of widespread political apathy. However, the evidence on working-class radicalism versus authoritarianism is very difficult to sort out because of the significance of leadership and "conditions" in determining consciousness. Mills's critique of leadership was unorthodox; the misfortune is that he never concentrated on the exact interaction between leaders and led to discover the actual "cooptation process" and how it might have been broken—that is, how the latent radicalism could become manifest. Therefore, on the whole, his work lapsed into the common and one-sided view of mass behavior in the 1950s while also containing the less common imputation of at least some substantial blame to leadership.

In one other decisive area, however, Mills fell into the orthodox descriptive and analytic categories. He treated poverty and racism as though they were nonexistent. For whatever reasons he did this (and none of any convincing substance have been advanced), he clearly reflected the prevailing tone of discussion and criticism in the postwar years in this respect. If it is a mystery why Mills neglected these areas; it is just as much or more a mystery why they were forgotten by American society altogether. These were years of intense jubilation over America's rising prosperity and the "income revolution"; what poverty remained was isolated and disappearing, not basic to the American system, or so the fable went.

As a matter of fact, however, poverty in America was becoming more comprehensive and severe with each year of the 1950s. It embraced all of Appalachia and most of the South; the centers of northern cities and much of the farm belt outside the South. It victimized the Negroes, Indians, Puerto Ricans, and Mexicans; the very old and very young; the unemployed and many of the insecurely employed. In 1956, the year that *The Power Elite* was published, the Bureau of the Census counted 35 percent of U.S. families under $3,000 and 47 percent under $4,000 income—yet the Department of Labor then estimated that families of four needed $4,300 to live at a "minimum standard of decency."

In a similar sense, the status of Negroes was hardly to be celebrated. World War II seemed to bring a permanent advance by opening up thousands of semiskilled occupations in northern industry to Negroes migrating up from the South. The national ideology, and policy, moreover, seemed more bent in the direction of civil rights than ever before: there was the war against the Nazi radical ideology, the abolition of the white-only primary in 1944, the desegregation of the armed forces in 1948, and the climactic 1954 school desegregation decision. The wave of anticolonial revolutions in the international scene, moreover, brought important indirect pressure on American leadership in the direction of desegregation.

Thus it became commonplace to take an optimistic view that poverty and discrimination, if not erased, were problems being confronted successfully. That Mills took this view is doubtful—he was hardly an optimist about the United States—but it is clear that at least it was one of the few instances where he failed to attack a dominant myth. This failure was more than an oversight;

it fundamentally crippled his analysis of capitalist stabilization, the prospect for social change, and his own role as a radical.

One year after the release of *The Power Elite,* Rosa Parks took her seat at the front of a bus in Montgomery, Alabama. From what evidence exists, she might fit most of the terms of the mass society analysis. She was a Negro, and for that she was refused her seat. In a matter of days, the Montgomery Improvement Association was created, and shortly afterward the Rev. Martin Luther King came to international prominence as an apostle of revolutionary Christianity and nonviolence in America. In the years following, the movement was to enlarge and spread constantly, finally involving Negroes of the North as well as the South, lower class as well as middle class, and to intensify with protest the already serious unemployment and poverty problems facing the United States. That Mills must have been somewhat unimpressed with this revolt is clear when it is contrasted to his response to the Cuban Revolution. He journeyed to Cuba, prepared himself with exhausting study and interviewing, and wrote a flaming book to Americans from the point of view of a hypothesized Cuban revolutionary. But he never made a trip south to investigate the brewing racial crisis.

The civil rights revolution still is lacking a solid theoretical explanation—and this is not the place to make that attempt. What is important, however, is to understand how the civil rights crisis suggests modifications in Mills's analysis.

In stressing the manipulative capacity and degree of stable integration of the power elite, Mills tended to underemphasize the role of "backward capitalism" in creating crises within corporate capitalism. "Backward capitalism" is meant to describe two specific phenomena: (1) small businessmen and independent producers whose *structure* requires low costs, antiunion practices, and so forth; and (2) major corporations still characterized by "backward" social *attitudes.* Mills correctly described the first group as the "petty right," but it was never clear that he included the second group in this category; indeed, the most reasonable interpretation is that he included corporations in the "corporate rich" sector of the power elite. He seriously underestimated the degree to which certain American industrial capitalists hold negative views toward the welfare and broker roles assumed by the state. Even though a variety of "liberal" policies could be adopted to improve the conditions of the Negroes and the poor without altering big property interests, these corporate ideologues oppose any further extension of the welfare state. They adopt, with small businessmen and the rest of the "petty right," the characteristic attitude summarized in Kaysen et al.'s survey of American Business creeds: "[The role of the government in the economy should be] the maintenance of law and order through the enforcement of the criminal law; the law of torts; the enforcement of contracts; the regulation of the health and safety of the population; the licensing of the professions; the conservation of natural resources; the provision of education; and the relief of distress."

To be concrete, racism, arbitrary exploitation, and antiunionism are characteristic of many businesses in the American South; and these practices are condoned, at least tacitly and often explicitly, by big northern business. It was predictable that the civil rights movement would emerge first in the region where the welfare corporatism of the power elite has been least successful in replacing these traditional market arrangements. The frustration, through racism, of middle-class Negro professional hopes, coupled with the destruction of Negro laborers by the mechanization of farming, backed by constant police state tactics, were the underlying conditions pushing Negroes of all classes in the South to a point of revolt.

Perhaps Mills missed this crisis because he was so alienated from orthodox liberal issues and so intent on pointing to the "silent conservative" as the real enemy rather than the "petty right." Perhaps he was so engrossed in the theory of a stabilized American political economy that he regarded "backward capitalism" as a lag instead of an Achilles' heel.

A kind of indirect evidence for this lies in the fact that he spent only a few lines in analyzing what was considered the major domestic political phenomenon of the early 1950s—Mc-Carthyism. As with racism, McCarthyism was not the orientation of the power elite. It was the policy of certain dispossessed socioeconomic groups and an expression of decline, not of ascendance. Indeed, it is rather indisputable that these were not the intended policies of the big corporations, the military, and the political diplomats; and, as will be seen, Mills's great virtue precisely lay in his ability to see the "higher immorality" at a time when most intellectuals were viewing racism as a disappearing blemish and McCarthyism as the consummate threat to society and themselves. But the shortcoming in Mills's analysis, too, was in his failure to see the chance for the politics and publics, which he wanted so badly, in the very issues of racism and poverty he neglected. He saw that the international focus of the 1940s and 1950s was instrumental to the entrenchment of the power elite; he did not see how domestic crisis and insurgency could return national attention to the American society and thereby threaten the power of the elite. It is not merely the racial problem that now is having this effect, but rather the whole question of poverty. From a theoretical viewpoint again, the existence of poverty is a direct product of the imperfect and incomplete evolution of corporatism in which the political state has failed to function in its assigned role as the stabilizing guarantor for those whose needs have not been met by the workings of the private sector.

It is only slightly an oversimplification to point out that the "welfare state revolution" ended in the late 1930s, and, since that time, liberal legislation has been hollowed out or consistently defeated by congressional reactionaries. The social security, welfare assistance, minimum wage, and workmen's and unemployment compensation laws still do not cover the neediest, and they are inadequate for those who receive them. These programs, according to Harrington, "were designed for the middle third in the cities, for the organized workers, and for the upper third in the country, for the big market farmers.... [The welfare state] was stimulated by mass impoverishment and misery, yet it helped the poor least of all."

Harrington and Galbraith have stressed the fact of the political invisibility of the current poor. Harrington writes that they do not

> belong to unions, to fraternal organizations, or to political parties. They are without lobbies of their own; they put forward no legislative program. As a group they are atomized. They have no face; they have no voice.... Because the slums are no longer centers of powerful political organization, the politicians need not really care about their inhabitants.

Thus the "reforms" subsequent to the New Deal were even less palpable than those of the 1930s: The 1946 Full Employment Act contrasts with the successive increases in unemployment after each of the postwar recessions; the 1949 Housing Act authorized 810,000 units of public housing by 1953, but by 1963 only 500,000 units were constructed, and mostly at rental costs too high for the neediest.

Mills unfortunately "transcended" these issues; after the study of Puerto Ricans, he never again scrutinized the lower sections of the "mass society," nor did he describe in a detailed way the issues being debated at the "middle levels of power." With his attention taken by international crises and the stabilizing power of the new elite, he failed to observe the domestic stagnation in social services that accompanied the building of the "permanent war economy." With his attention taken by the decline of politics to the middle levels of power, he overlooked the ways in which Congress, through its own default, was creating the segregated and impoverished conditions for protest. With his attention taken by the "crackpot realism" of foreign policy, he missed its domestic counterpart: If the power elite was so sophisticated, so manipulative, why did it permit the gross deterioration of American domestic conditions in the postwar period?

These gaps prevented Mills from making a quite early, and therefore quite original, analysis of automation and the defense economy. In *The Power Elite,* he pointed out that automation

would permit greater centralized control by the means of production. It neglected the human effects, however, especially
the profit-inspired introduction of automated equipment as
a "labor-saving" device. This process, which is just becoming
recognized as a critical problem in the 1960s, is eliminating the
need for Negroes and whites in nearly all skill categories in the
mass-production sectors, and in this decade it is beginning to
enter white-collar areas as well. The proximate origin of this
"cybernation revolution," it is quite important to note, was in the
World War II expansion of scientific research at public expense.
The introduction of automated equipment, therefore, was not
felt during the giddy period of the postwar boom or during the
years in which the Korean War kept employment needs relatively
high. Ironically, the real impact of automation began just after
Mills's attention was turning away from analysis of the American scene. While Mills discussed the "sociological imagination,"
Cuba, the causes of World War III, and historical Marxism, the
American productive system was being transformed. More than
half the new jobs created from 1957 on were in the public sector,
mostly in teaching. Of the 4.3 million jobs created during those
years, only 200,000 were established through the sole efforts of
the private sector. Aggravating the problem was a massive influx
of individuals into the labor market of the 1950s, the offspring
of the war years. A controversial Senate subcommittee in 1964
concluded that even to hold unemployment at presently unac-
ceptable levels, an additional $5 billion must be spent annually
in the public sector.

Of course, this situation strikes at Negroes severely—that
is why the racial and economic crises are superimposed. What
"progress" Negroes made was in the 1940–1951 period when
the median Negro family income rose from 40 to 54 percent of
the median white family income—but this was due largely to
the South-to-North migration that brought Negroes into a less
impoverished geographic area and into nondiscriminatory war
industries, while keeping them in the same *relative* status. Negro
unemployment has risen from 8 percent in the "boom" to 13

percent today (while the figure for whites has lifted from about 4.5 percent to 6 percent).

The recent history of the civil rights movement involves a shift in constituency that reflects these problems—the initial middle-class professionals have been supplemented by industrial workers, the urban unemployed, and rural sharecroppers. This shift is reflected in programmatic change; from demands for desegregation of the social structure to the demand for structural change to permit job creation.

This was the first crisis Mills missed: the organic connection between a do-nothing Congress, profit-induced cybernation, racial discrimination, and poverty. Here are the seeds of a major liberal upsurge along the lines of the populist and labor revolts of the past. Such a movement, as it now is taking shape, pressures for a change in the priorities that for two decades placed the cold war above domestic needs.

The most obvious target of such pressures will be the defense economy—a fact that Mills would have anticipated brilliantly had he understood the racial upheaval. In *The Causes of World War Three,* Mills was the first to see that the changes in military technology were going to negate the stimulus role of the permanent war economy. He wrote that

> the new weaponry, the new kinds of war preparations, do not seem to be as economically relevant to subsidizing the defaults and irrationalities of the capitalist economy as the old armament preparations. The amount of money spent is large enough, but it tends to go to a smaller proportion of employees, to the technicians rather than the semi-skilled. The people who make missiles and bombs will probably not put into consumption as high a ratio of their incomes as would the more numerous makers of tanks and aircraft. Accordingly, the new type of military pump-priming will not prime as much; it will not carry as great a multiplier effect; it will not stimulate consumption or subsidize capitalism as well as the older type. It is a real capitalist difficulty, and the military expenditures may indeed have to be great to overcome it.

Indeed, military expenditures climbed 25 percent in the five years after these words were written; but the additional funds, spent on missiles and refined hardware, research and development, aggravated the problems Mills cited. By the 1960s, defense spending went most heavily to just a handful of states, more than half of American scientists and engineers were concentrated in defense to the neglect of civilian industry, and the war economy had collapsed as a full-employment mechanism.

Moreover, this failure was intimately related to the poverty and racial crises. With defense utilizing $60 billion of the $100 billion national budget (actually, 85 percent of all federal purchases of goods and services), it has been easy for conservatives to argue against "more welfare spending." With the shift in defense industry to skilled employees, especially engineers, the general employment problem has been left to deepen. Thus the defense emphasis has meant the curtailment of social service and the diversion of resources from civilian domestic needs. A basis has been laid for political action and debate about racial justice, America's unmet economic needs, and the stagnating effect of the arms race. This base is just today becoming evident. Civil rights, labor, and Democratic Party groups speak of these linkages increasingly. The 1963 March on Washington called for "*jobs and freedom*"; Negro leaders privately and publicly are eyeing the arms budget as a source of needed funds. Spokespeople for a national farm organization publicly call for cuts of as much as $20 billion from the defense sector; so, too, does the head of a national organization of the aged. Senators and Defense Department officials, too, speak of the leveling off and eventual decline of the arms expenditures. And would Mills have believed that even the *New York Times* would call for, in early 1964, a diversion of money from the cold war to President Johnson's War on Poverty?

This atmosphere of change is not confined to the domestic sphere alone—Mills did not see the approaching transformation of the cold war. If technological change and social protest were the gathering forces of change in the Untied States, their importance was dramatically magnified on the world scene. First, the postwar American role as "banker and policeman of the West" (the phrase is Walter Lippmann's) is terminating. Protected by American policy for the decade after World War II, the planned corporate economies of Europe were thriving by the late 1950s. Fully able to use their scientific personnel for modernization purposes while protected under the American defense umbrella, many of the industries, in Japan as well as Europe, are now competitively equal or superior to American enterprise. At the same time, the quest for military and political independence from America is gaining on the continent: from this perspective, Charles de Gaulle is not an aberrant figure but a logical production of reconstructed capitalist Europe.

At the same time, in the other cold war bloc, the ideological divisions between Russia and China are forcing new definitions of world conflict. Instead of the collapse of communism anticipated by the American establishment, the new scene suggests the rapid development of the kind of crisis for which the U.S. government often is unprepared. Not only is China, for instance, a form of communism for which America is unprepared, but its revolution reflects also the force of the anticolonial revolutions that have taken place in the last twenty years, culminating toward the beginning of the 1960s. These national social revolutions, by now becoming politically if not economically free of the West, inevitably create problems and pressure points independent of the traditional cold war interaction of Russia and the United States. It is apparent that the cold war, with its military and economic drain on the participants (Russia more so than the United States), is an impediment to safely facing the issues that now are emergent: If American priorities deny the American poor, they tenfold deny the world poor. If the American poor, except for the Negroes, are thus far quiescent in the face of this denial, the world's poor are actively bitter.

These changes in the configuration of world power relations have been accompanied by the declining utility of thermonuclear weapons. Despite a continuing commitment to "peace through strength," American leaders have become increasingly aware of two disabling effects of the weapons of total destruction. First, the U.S. nuclear arsenal does not effectively deter social revolution in the third world (after years of fearing a Red Army attack on Europe, American officials are discovering now that the focus of trouble is changing). Second, the bomb is becoming dysfunctional because of the inevitable spread of nuclear weapons to other countries. Thus certain key trends observed by Mills are seemingly reversed.

Europe, once devastated, is independently powerful.

Communist societies have increased and are as factionally sundered as the West.

Nuclear might was to be America's final security; now it haunts American statesmen.

The underdeveloped countries were subordinate; now they are a massive political force in world history.

America was the supposed model of a just and democratic form of development; now America is racked with racial and economic crisis.

The defense economy was a permanent prop; now it is an ever-heavier drag.

America was drugged with apathy; now America is split with debate.

A new era emerged to visible existence in the last few years. As with past epochal transitions, no one can be held responsible for not discerning its development. Only the bold outlines are apparent: (1) cybernation makes abundance possible with drastically less labor of the traditional manual type; (2) social revolution prepares the grave of white racism and economic exploitation; (3) nuclear technology makes general war an irrational instrument of policy.

Had Mills lived, he would barely have recognized the American scene. In his later writings, especially on the New Left, he idealized the emergence from apathy by students and young intellectuals in the South and around the world, but he failed to tie this to changing social and structural conditions. Had he lived, who knows what role would be his? This cannot be known, but we can ask whether his fundamental concept of the power elite is modified or undermined by the "data" of the new era. A strong case can be made that the racial and poverty problems are "soluble" within the general framework of political economy. By this reasoning, Mills might have drawn a parallel between the 1930s when, in the face of a crisis brought on by the petty right, the sophisticated conservatives moved in with their program for a corporate state. Their idea was only partially realized in the 1930s, and the need for it was reduced by the peculiar (counterrevolutionary) role of World War II, the boom, and the Korean War. As social conflict grows again, therefore, it is likely that the new insurgents will be incorporated into a structure modified to satisfy their demands. The political welfare state would be completed. Planning would be legitimized and shared by government, business, labor, and consumer. As a rational alternative to the free market model, the government and the larger corporations would be established in interlocked harmony. Labor unions, their membership base shrunken, would occupy a formal but subordinate slot, perhaps eventually disappearing and being replaced by corporation subunits or "sections." Public assistance would be more broadly extended, and public education as well, for a healthy and technically skilled citizenry would be indispensable to such a fragile advanced system. Racism would be barred because of its uselessness.

Would this be a capitalist society? Not in the sense of an integration of ownership and management; but, strictly speaking, capitalist economies no longer have this form of integration even today. It would be capitalist, however, in the normative and legal sanction of private ownership, planning, and gain. Certainly such a system would retain an interest in dominative, though flexible, trade relations with the Third World, and it would oppose communist movements demanding public forms of ownership and control. Most important, Mills might argue, the material bases of injustice would be evaporated by this corporate society, leaving only the less clear problems of psychological oppression and maldistributed power with a materially contented public. Though the possibility of "socialism growing up within the framework of corporatism" (e.g., through the widespread experience of government spending for the public welfare), the possibility would rest on a very tenuous ground: the possibility of the majority of people demanding the power to control their own lives. This would be difficult to imagine because of the high levels of abundance and leisure, the difficulty in making clear the social causes of personal anxiety, and the American tradition of refusing to believe in the existence of uncontrolled power. It is true that the forms of capitalism grew up and became consciously revolutionary within feudal social order, but only because of material needs and perceived differences. The same would not hold true for the development of socialism in a welfare-corporatist society. Lenin and others saw this and argued consequently that "socialist construction" would have to take place *after* the revolution against private property. But this image of revolution—a polarization of classes, a transfer of power, followed by revolutionary construction—is no more realistic than the image in which the new society grows up within the forms of the old until finally the new forces outweigh the old. Are not both forms of revolution obviated by the capacity of the corporate state to create material satisfaction along with ideological confusion and conformity? This is what Mills meant in his fear about the "rise of the cheerful robot" as a social type in the advanced industrial countries.

This is a formidable possibility. It would permit Mills to argue that the defeat of the petty right could occur without changing the larger framework of private minority rule. He could even argue that the "military-industrial complex," or, specifically, the more scandalous profit-seeking defense contractors, would be politically defeated while leaving intact the Department of Defense, the Central Intelligence Agency, the paramilitary and counterguerilla bands, and the elite system of military decision making. In fact, this is a real possibility today, given the leveling off of defense spending and the rigid inability of most of the aerospace industry to convert to civilian markets. Just as this process is undercutting Boeing, North American, Republic, and the other big missile contractors, the United States has increased by sixfold its expenditure on antiguerilla operations in Southeast Asia, Latin America, and Africa. These "special forces" operations are inevitably on the side of conservative or reactionary elements in these new countries, and almost entirely outside the channels of democratic, even congressional, review. While the political arena echoes with debates on civil rights and poverty, the "proletariat" of the third world is being militarily, politically, and economically exploited by the United States. "Backward capitalism" remains the dominant fact of overseas economic relations, while corporate capitalism is becoming entrenched in the domestic sphere.

No one knows whether a struggle for power is likely to occur in an abundant society—there is no precedent, of course. This ambiguity, however, and the present "new insurgency" in America, do not negate Mills's thesis but only suggest questions and refinements of the theory of elite power wielding.

One refinement suggested, which should be reiterated, has to do with Mills's view of the agencies of change. Certainly his view of the potential insurgency of the masses and the working class was inadequate. It did not anticipate the present and potential movements for change in the United States.

Mills admitted, in the "Letter to the New Left" and elsewhere, that he was "not happy" with the idea of the intellectuals as the agency. Their role as an agency seemed often for him to be a defensive one, practicing reason and freedom by attempting to expose the power elite, the threat of war, the debasement of democratic institutions. Mills's view of the intellectuals in revolution was never really developed theoretically, in some part because their role was obviously not going to be revolutionary in the American situation. As he defined it several times, the American intellectual's concrete role was to speak flatly to three groups: (1) to the power elite, inputting blame and suggesting at least "safe" courses; (2) the unconsciously powerful, making them aware of their responsibilities and violated interests; (3) the unpowerful, creating publics and politics. He himself demonstrated what he meant, bringing out a series of books and essays: *The Sociological Imagination, The Cause of World War Three, Listen, Yankee, The Marxists,* "The New Left," "A Pagan Sermon for the Christian Clergy," "The Cultural Apparatus," "The Decline of the Left," and "On Reason and Freedom."

Only in the 1960s did Mills become at all enthusiastic about his thesis on the intellectuals, and even then in a way that reflected considerable sensitivity to trends. What he observed was the rapid upsurge of revolt "led" by young intellectuals, in the U.S. South, Cuba, Turkey, Taiwan, South Korea, Okinawa, Great Britain, and Japan. Mills suddenly thought the idea of the intellectuals as a positive, radical agency "might be very relevant indeed." Then, instead of "abandoning the working class," he wrote, "we've got to study these new generations of intellectuals around the world as real live agencies of historical change. Forget Victorian Marxism except whenever you need it; and read Lenin again (be careful)—Rosa Luxembourg too."

Cuba became symbolic of this New Left for Mills—and a specific cause of his terrible anguish about the American future. Here was a new beginning, and Mills spoke of it in the role of a Cuban revolutionary pleading for Americans to "listen." Much of the success of the revolution, he thought, could be attributed to young, middle-class intellectuals who were able to "make contact" with the Cuban peasantry, and later the urban wage workers. What excited Mills, and he might have exaggerated slightly, was the newness of the revolution. Whereas in 1948 he accepted, though with some suspicion, the "independent left" view of unions and third parties, here he was able to set it aside with glee. "Our revolution is not a revolution made by labor unions or wage workers in the city, or by labor parties, or by anything like that. It is far from any revolution you ever heard of before."

The intellectuals, he thought, were also important because of their stress on culture and education as the source of Cuban freedom in the long struggle. But what excited him most was the practical and humane approach of the revolution in the

1956–1960 period. The key, it seemed to him, was that these were revolutionaries of the post-Stalin era, not of the old left intelligentsia, never having lived through early dogmatism and later disillusion. Here Mills fell into bitter differences: with the liberals who insisted on constitutional democracy right away in Cuba; the democratic socialists who went further and called him an apologist for totalitarianism; the pro-communist left that was irked by his description of the party as being to the "right of the revolution" in Cuba.

At about the same time, Mills began his identification with the European and specifically British "New Left"—a new generation of writers and activists concerned with new forms of thought and action. The radical was beginning to find comrades—after a long, long journey. But the fact that he could not find them in the United States points to a final necessary element in understanding Mills's work. He discovered new conditions wherever he looked: a new elite dominating a new domestic and world situation; a mass society emerging after the political promise of the 1930s; class conflict little more than a metaphysical fact, so deeply was it buried in the new managerialism; and, finally, the nearly complete absence of opposition or protest groups within American society. This last fact completed the circle of his and perceived isolation, and it is the final matter to be examined in an intellectual biography of Mills.

Chapter 3

The Radical Nomad and the New Left

Mills never had a base. That is not just a significant biographical fact but one that signifies much about these times. His alienation from the intellectual community was only one part of his malaise. Probably the larger alienation was political: there was no ideology, no movement, no party was "home." He felt Marxism and liberalism were theoretically exhausted: both stemmed from the Enlightenment equation of reason with freedom, leading to the assumption that people eventually will take *personal* interest in their "objective" interest. Moreover, both ideologies were becoming self-serving and conservative defenses for the power elites of the United States and USSR. Not only was existing ideology inadequate, but there was no community of people with whom Mills could work as a "comrade." There was no American Left; there had not been one genuinely rooted in American experience since the Socialist Party of 1900–1919.

But what was more paralyzing, and historically unusual, was the disappearance of reform causes and political life in general. In the 1940s and 1950s political consensus so dominated political cleavage as to make it almost vain to plot a right-to-left continuum for American politics, even within the framework of the "middle levels of power." Politically, liberalism was less and less distinguishable from the center, or what Mills called the "main drift" in 1948. He formed his mature theories, in short, not only out of the experience of World War II, the boom, the cold war, and the new military and industrial elites but also out of the demise of the liberal-left and with it, political debate.

The rampant signs of new politics in the 1960s were not sensed in depth by Mills, though his death came just at their inception. He was adroit enough, however, to sense the prospect for a "new left," based primarily in the third world countries but also within the two big power blocs. This dying conception was very crucial but cannot be understood without some examination of the crisis of liberal and Marxian social thought, and the decline of liberal and left politics in the United States since the New Deal.

As a radical intellectual, the crisis for Mills was not of the end of ideological thinking but the end of comprehensive revolutionary ideology. In *The Marxists,* but in earlier works as well, he stressed a need to "get beyond" Marxism, especially to take into account the development of effectively independent political and military elites and to shape a new theory of the agencies of change. A constant theme was that of finding the "necessary conditions" of free human self-consciousness, from the practical crisis of the Cuban Revolution to the macrocrisis of the advanced industrial nations. This he felt Marxism lacked, because of the assumption that class needs will be perceived accurately and acted upon. Despite this, he basically respected Marxian thought because of its comprehensive and dynamic sweep as a method of studying history-in-motion. And on these grounds he estimated it more highly than liberalism as a philosophy and strategy for humanism. While liberalism embodied the same ideals, it lacked a theory of change. It rested on the proposed equilibrium of voluntary associations that Mills perceived as actually attenuating, instead of liberating, the faculty of reason. And beyond this, liberalism shared Marxism's fundamental disadvantage of assuming rationality.

If interpreted rather strictly, in terms of the nineteenth century or specifically in terms of Marx and Engels, Jeremy Bentham, and John Stuart Mill, this analysis was both valid and orthodox.

What was originally insightful with Mills was the implication that he developed to fit the larger outlines of his work. The crisis of political anxiety and indifference stems precisely from the use of reason to manipulate false needs and consciousness, to contain class conflict, to rationalize vested interests. In these circumstances, the common humanist ideals of both creeds are adapted to the purposes of two inhuman systems. The source of much of Mills's futility, not always a conscious source, was in his inability to do more than practice reason and freedom himself in an effort to expose and educate.

His search for new ideological clarity ended unfinished. He had made tentative conclusions about the viability of humanist ideals, the prospect for a new agency of change, and structure and process in the "over" and "underdeveloped" societies. But he was fundamentally worried about his theory, especially the question of historical agencies. He tagged himself a "plain Marxist" finally, as opposed to the "orthodox Marxists." But even this was as much a mood as a distinct point of view, and it carried with it the feeling that Marxism, though crucial, was not comprehensive enough.

Mills's plain Marxism (1) sees Marx as a great nineteenth-century figure, in undogmatic terms; (2) sees Marxism as a tradition with historically specific significance; (3) politically, is a "loser's ideology." Plain Marxists "may have been through the Party, of one sort or another, yet as plain Marxists they have stood outside it; they have not been enchurched." It also (4) stresses the humanism of Marx, especially of the 1844 *Manuscripts*; (5) stresses the role of the "superstructure" in history as an area of influence for better or, more often, for worse; (6) stresses that "'economic determinism' is, after all, a matter of degree, and holds that it is so used by Marx in his own writings, especially in his historical essays"; (7) stresses the "volition of men in making history—their freedom—in contrast to any Determinist law of History and accordingly, the lack of individual responsibility"; (8) "confronts the unresolved tension in Marx's work—and in history itself: the tension of humanism and determinism, or human freedom and historical necessity."

If there was a common quality in these precepts, it was radical honesty and integrity. Here, of course, plain Marxists joined with what one could call "plain liberalism," with its emphasis on inquiry and discussion. It was primarily on this point that Mills's theory and practice joined, and where he felt estranged from left and liberal orthodoxies everywhere in the world. "In our time there is no left establishment anywhere that is truly international and insurgent—and at the same time, consequential."

Mills criticized the failure of the Soviet Union to develop a real and legal basis for opposition and free debate. He was critical of communist parties almost everywhere for their "smugness" and "apologetics."

The more consuming revulsion as an American, however, was with liberalism. The socialist and communist movements in the United States had been whittled down, at least as independent forces, on the American scene by 1950, defeated by their own orientation to the Soviet bloc rather than the American experience. Mills's acrimony was directed, therefore, at the liberal and social-democratic forces, specifically the leadership stratum of the labor, civil rights, and peace movement activists, northern reform-Democratic politicians, and writers and intellectuals around magazines such as *The Nation, New Republic, Commentary, Encounter, Partisan Review,* and *Dissent.*

The history of this liberalism effectively began in the New Deal where many currently established liberals spent their youth in radical left-wing movements. Out of the New Deal came a great achievement, the final incorporation of labor as a legitimate, if limited, enterprise in the American political economy. Whether the labor movement, having been established, would have renewed any radicalism again in the early 1940s was a question eliminated by the nationalistic pressures of World War II. The war brought with it a decline in the widespread social dissent that had characterized the 1930s, and the labor leadership was among the chief groups loyal to the national interest, as defined by business and government, during the war years. This was partly because of the deep fear of German fascism and belief in the superior worth of the American system in part, but in some sense it was also because of the "status anxieties" natural to a former out-group that recently had become socially legitimate. In the wake of the war came the construction of the main institutions that Mills confronted in his writings. The cold war developed, inter-nationalized the threat of social upheaval that had been expected to arise from domestic tensions. The major resources—human and technological—were geared to the policies of strengthening anticommunist forces and containing "subversive" movements around the world. This became a domestic worry as well, though in a form aberrant from the executive policy, in McCarthyism.

But simultaneous with this worry over domestic and inter-national betrayal came a wide-shared sense of satisfaction with the workings of the American system. An atmosphere of confi-dence in national viability replaced the fear of breakdown that had been so rampant in the 1930s and 1940s. The chief point of national pride was the private or "mixed" economy that seemed, for once and for all, a stable repository of national abundance. This enthusiasm was the expression not just of big-businessmen but of most of the vocal liberal, ex-insurgent community as well. This feeling was rather obvious in the works, for instance, of the dozen social scientists who put out a study of the *New American Right* that analyzed America as an abundant society ridden with status, rather than class, tensions. It was a durable mood, too; for instance, Robert Hutchins, president of the Center for the Study of Democratic Institutions, declared as late as 1958:

> The nature and scope of the present crisis would seem to justify sustained thought and discussion about how to cope with it. In the United States, and in many other parts of the West, *almost all the goals of the nineteenth century reformers have been achieved,* all of them, in fact, except peace. We have education, information, wealth, leisure, and democracy. But the earthly paradise eludes us still.

This national self-satisfaction, as we have seen, had an unstable basis in fundamentally abnormal conditions. The needs that produced the boom—defense of the Free World, reconstruction of sagging European economies, fulfillment of a backlog of consumer demands that had developed since 1929, the use of corporate savings for plant modernization and expansion—were not seen as transitory. The lesson most people learned, instead, was that high and permanent levels of prosperity, and relative justice, were the achievements of the same state capitalism that had been maligned in the 1930s.

As conservative trends came to dominance, within the liberal-labor movement a crippling struggle went on. The cold war had gripped the house of labor. In 1945, the American Communist Party controlled unions that contained one-fourth of the entire CIO membership. A cruel struggle for power began in the CIO, in many instances a carryover of intense communist-anticommunist struggles of the 1930s. The conflict involved not simply intraunion issues but national political ones as well: whether to accept or reject noncommunist affidavits as a prerequisite to service from the National Labor Relations Board; whether to support or oppose the Marshall Plan; and whether to support the Democrats, Socialists, or Progressives in 1948. At the end of five years of combat, the CIO expelled every suspect union. For many labor leaders, a majority of whom had fought communism since the 1930s or who had left the party to become rigid anti-communists, the experience and tactics of the late 1940s would mark their vision indelibly with a fear of political associations or of involvement in ventures where communist infiltration might occur. This was linked usually to an acceptance of the rightness of the West, however blemished, and the necessity for a national defense economy of constantly expanding proportion.[1] This remained true, for example, through the late 1950s. It was a segregationist southern Democrat, Jamie Whitten, who was calling 30 percent of the defense budget waste at one point while the Americans for Democratic Action were proclaiming in their budgetary analysis, "surely we agree that the security needs of the United States must be met despite the cost."

Thus, one critical ingredient of the times that created the established liberalism of the 1950s was the "arrival" of the labor movement as a functional part of the corporation-dominated economy. Power was achieved with the invisible "stipulation" that the voice of labor would not be a radical one. Labor was to function as a veto group, and a minority one in industrial relations, and not as the irritating seed of a different social order.

The second ingredient in the making of liberalism was the bitter fight over communism, which both weakened the Left in endless internal struggles and sent many into a flight for security against the widely used McCarthyist red smear.

The third was the relative improvement of American conditions in general after several decades of instability. The founding of the Americans for Democratic Action (ADA) in the 1940s was a key instance of tending to act politically *against* the communist threat instead of acting primarily *on behalf* of positive social values. Speaking at a House of Representatives investigation in 1950, ADA national chairman Frances Biddle explained the reasons for beginning his organization four years earlier:

> Really the ADA was largely founded to split from the liberal movement in America those elements of communism and fellow-travellers which in my opinion—certainly up until 1945—did great harm to the liberal movement by permitting, with some justice, the accusation of fellow-travellers before the sheep and the goats had been counted.

ADA provided a framework in which liberals could act publicly with a fair chance of not being destroyed in smear campaigns. Anticommunist disclaimers were perceived as necessary—indeed, were fetishized—among liberals attempting to be "effective" in a growing atmosphere of suspicion. A part of the national suspiciousness, too, was generated by ADA leaders themselves in their own domestic struggles to diminish "communist" influence in national circles. Looking back at that period, with perhaps an exaggerated notion of ADA's own practice of fully democratic principles, attorney Joseph ("Mr. ADA") Rauh wrote:

> ADA promptly set to work to fight communism at home and abroad. It was at first a bitter and uphill struggle. In every place where they had established themselves, the communists fought back ruthlessly, through their favored devices of secret conspiracy and character assassination. We made ourselves for a time very unpopular with a large number of well-meaning but innocent people who could not see that communists ... constituted a danger to our democracy.

Hubert Humphrey, one of their founders and pillars, supported the anticommunist Subversive Activities Control Act in 1950 and amended it with the Communist Control Act of 1953, making it impossible for a visible Communist Party to legitimately exist in America. But America proved not very grateful to ADA for its work in eliminating the "communist conspiracy," and in ADA there soon appeared the deep defensiveness typical of organized liberal efforts of the 1950s. "With no real communist movement around and about," wrote Rauh, "we represented the 'furthest out' tendency in practical American politics—and were promptly called every name in the dictionary for the 'crime' of having successfully fought the communists."

While ADA was turning itself into a relatively minor lobbying force pleading with conservative officialdom, many of the individuals who were "fringe radicals" during the 1930s become loyal, often quiescent and satisfied, social reformers. At one time disaffected from organized society, their social ties became multiple and overlapping as they fought for power: they were integrated deeply into the status quo while attempting to change it. Walter Reuther, a revolutionary in the early 1930s, became a respected part of the American establishment by the late 1950s. Daniel Bell, a fighting member of the Young People's Socialist League at age thirteen, finally became labor editor for *Fortune* magazine. Thousands of others, affected by prosperity or McCarthyism or personal problems, opted out of social struggle altogether. Organized liberalism, in one sense, became the *residue* of the great and unfulfilled movements of the 1920s and 1930s.

One final ingredient was important, however: the virtual absence of independent insurgent movements for change "from below" in the 1940s and 1950s. Without this, the liberal organizations were making appeals to the centers of power without pressure from disadvantaged groups and classes. It became all too easy to be caught up in the fantasies of power politics, in the illusion of real influence, and in the retreat from a militant pursuit of ideals in a situation basically overweighted to the conservative side. The liberal rhetoric became what Mills termed an "administrative rationale":

> In close contact with power, liberalism has become more administrative and less political. It has become practical, flexible, realistic, pragmatic—as liberals assert—and not at all utopian. All of which means, I think, that as an ideology, as a rhetoric, liberalism has often become irrelevant to political positions having moral content.

Mills's own "sociology of liberalism" was left incomplete, though he did periodically attack the role its leadership had played since the New Deal:

> Postwar liberalism has been organizationally impoverished: the pre-war years of liberalism-in-power devitalized independent liberal groups, drying up their grass-roots, making older leaders dependent on the federal center and not training new leaders around the country. The New Deal left no liberal organization to carry on any liberal program; rather than a new party, its instrument was a loose coalition inside the old one, which quickly fell apart as far as liberal ideas are concerned.... In their moral fright, postwar liberals have not defended any left-wing or even militantly liberal position.

But liberalism, of course, was not simply organizational; it also developed characteristic moral and social outlooks, and it was against these also that Mills sharply resisted.

The dominant liberal notion, expressed in numerous ways, was a pessimism about democracy as a way of life in which the people participate actively to control their shared resources. At the core of this pessimism was a prudent estimate of human potentialities.

One stream of this thinking concentrated on the problems of "mass society." Prosperous America was seen to be endangered by a steadily deteriorating culture. This was not thought to be the result of capitalism or other social causes traditionally cited by left-wing sociology, but the unique product of a rich culture that had advanced technically far ahead of its lagging mores of perception, tastes, and interests. For many political intellectuals, the 1952 defeat of Adlai Stevenson symbolized the beginnings of ascendance of the uncivil mob over the cultured, delicate, and urbane minority. "The people," once sanctified in the struggles of the 1930s, were turned on and blamed for being "lowbrow" or "mass" or "base." An insightful summary of this general tendency was provided by the political theorist Sheldon Wolin:

> The juxtaposition of mass and elite is highly informative of the present state of theorizing, for it discloses that contemporary theory is, in a special sense, post-Marxian, and in terms of mood, disenchanted.... Instead of the highly self-conscious proletariat, the proud bearers of man's historical destiny, history has given us the vulgar mass; instead of Adonis, Quasimodo.

The truly captivating intellectual mood, and a justification for personal departures from a radical past, were provided by the doctrine of "the end of ideology." Given fullest expression by Bell, Shils, Lipset, and a variety of intellectuals around the then-blossoming Committee for Cultural Freedom, this point of view declared the dangers of moral enthusiasm and the exhaustion of Marxian ideology. It asserted that the West had solved most of its essential problems and now was challenged from within by totalitarian communism. Lipset's argument was typical:

Democracy is not only or even primarily a means through which different groups can attain their ends or seek the good society; it is the good society itself in operation.... The ideological issues dividing left and right have been reduced to a little more or less government ownership and economic planning. [This] reflects the fact that the fundamental political problems of the industrial revolution have been solved: the workers have achieved industrial and political citizenship; the conservatives have accepted the welfare state; and the democratic left has recognized that an increase in overall state power carries with it more dangers to freedom than solutions for economic problems.

From this position, politicians and some intellectuals were criticized for being too rigid or unwilling to compromise, or for their fear of impurity. It pointed always to fascism, and especially to Stalinism, as the likely results of ideological or moral rigidity. Shils was proud of the "positive standards of action inherent in our present attachment to moderation in action and orderliness and stability in change."

The CIA-supported Committee on Cultural Freedom's 1955 Milan conference on "The Future of Freedom" was marked, in Shils's opinion, by the atmosphere of a "post-victory ball": "There was in a variety of ways, a sometimes rampant, sometimes quiet conviction that communism had lost the battle of ideas with the West." These sentiments found religious expression primarily in the neo-orthodoxy of Reinhold Niebuhr, whose radical optimism of the 1930s had become, by the 1950s, a fear of the "depravities" inherent in man. In either its secular or religious formulation, this profound liberal wariness dominated the thought of the times, making traditional notions such as "the infinite potentialities of men," class conflict, or even the absolute defense of the first amendment (by using it in controversial ways, or by defending communist rights of association) seem quaint and outmoded.

Implicit in this liberal outlook was a defense of "pluralist society." This kind of social order, defined by its ability to prevent any single group from becoming irresponsibly dominant, was seen as a special American blessing. Riesman, Schlesinger, Parsons, and Galbraith were among the main ideologues of this new self-regulating order in which reform and change were viewed as necessary, although possible through a gradual and adaptive process. The American system, in this view, was seen as containing all the requirements of the good life for everyone, as well as means of attaining that life. The system was infinitely resourceful, and anything reasonable could be achieved by orderly means. Passionate action, especially where it involves the unstructured activity of millions of persons, was seen as extremely dangerous—though sometimes justifiable where an employer or bigot is being reactionary, a trend that supposedly was declining in the new managerial system.

Because of this distrust of the masses, the strain of organizational complexity, the felt need for efficiency, and the sense that the modern political economy had made irrelevant the traditional "left versus right" debates, many liberals went along with the enlarging world of bureaucracy. The modern conservative may be correct when he complains of the liberal acceptance of big government, but for incorrect reasons. The conservative who seeks a return to the world of small business is trapped in the contradiction of also advocating a large defense establishment that requires a big government. The liberal, on the other hand, accepts largeness in organizations. Bazelon claims, for instance, that "the liberal middlebrows are the vanguard of the managerial revolution in this country.... They are well placed in all the intellectual activities—foundations, mass culture in all forms, governmental bureaus—and seem to be making out, though more slowly, in the corporate bureaucracies as well."

What Bazelon has called a "contempt for disbelief in the forms of political democracy" leads to the attitude that "power in a government controlled by voters is more to be deplored than power in a corporate system not so controlled." For this reason, and because of the apparent impossibility of mobilizing opposition to the corporations, the liberals have endorsed the growth of the modern corporate economy and searched for ways to humanize and enlighten it. Occasionally populist ardor bursts through in an attack on corporate privilege, but on the whole there has been an acceptance of the size and power of the corporation, its ability to mobilize opinion, set social priorities, manipulate small businesses and individual employees, and crucially influence American foreign policy.

A way of thinking has been developed that permits corporate extravaganzas to go unnoticed—along with other injustices of the society. From the pluralist notion of a society in magic balance and self-adjustment flow two main liberal concepts of social change. The first is that conflict is a product of misunderstanding or unfortunate accidents, not of tensions within a social structure. Politics, economics, and social change become personalized to the exclusion of relevant and impersonal social conditions. Differences, for example, between some members of NAACP branches and angry Negro youth are seen as differences between generations or as communication breakdowns, rather than as conflicts between a comfortable gentry and politically marginal groups with conflicting needs.

The second, and related, idea here is the disavowal of causality. The liberal often does not acknowledge the existence of decisive trends with causal effects. Such theorizing is rejected by continued reference to the complexity of issues. Causes are seen as too numerous, too interacting, too confused to give people a sensible and coherent picture of reality. Mills imaginatively characterized this tendency when he wrote, "Liberals have no convincing view of the structure of society as a whole—other than the now vague notion of it as some kind of big balance.... It is doubtful that liberalism is in a position to designate the conditions under which the ideals it proclaims might be realized." Thus liberalism tended to reject not only historical inevitability but also the pursuit of understanding central happenings in history and the expectation of sudden and rough change.

The root problem, perhaps, is that liberalism regularly blurs the meaning of freedom. It is usually believed that people more often than not are really determining their own lives. Freedom means little more than that most people are doing what they seem to want to do. Those who are prevented from doing this are seen as either too selfish, as in the case of Robber Barons, or too extreme, as in the case of the pacifists who leap on submarines. Freedom rarely is seen as being defined by the way a society reacts to tests of its premises. Intrusions on personal freedom are seen as excesses committed by specific public officials, not as the self-preserving momentum of threatened interests. Being a reformer, the liberal thinks mostly of latitude within the system for rearrangements, less often in terms of the openness of the system to radical challenges. Freedom sometimes is equated with the existence of a broad civil liberties framework, and less frequently in relation to a subjective state of human consciousness in which one can see himself as he is with honesty. Nor has it much to do, in the liberal view, with the availability of structural vantage points from which people might see their society more truly than from their routinized, fragmented, and usually exploited everyday positions. Unused to analyzing life in terms of power, authority, and class—that is, in terms of the *likelihood of people being able to be free*—the liberal is too satisfied with the formal possibility of people being free. Finally, freedom does not often mean a quality of personality developed through involvement in a community of people but as a quality individually achieved and preserved.

This constellation of views, taken singly or together, is full of inadequacy—though there has been very little challenge to liberal ideology until recently. Mills's criticism of this ideology, taking its main lines of argument, shaped rebuttal to liberalism along these lines:

First, the flat and pessimistic image of man's potential is not one based on solid evidence, and, if it were, a respect for man's limits could more easily be converted into an argument for a new society where the institutions promote cooperation and rational rather than possessive individualism. Arguments for radical change—for instance, to socialism—need not be based on a utopian image of man as liberalism and conservativism often charge.

Second, the argument that pluralism prevails in the United States is not as convincing as the argument that pluralism exists within a dominant net of social institutions whose mutual interests are in preserving minority rule over the economy. The essential defense of a Galbraith or a Berle, for that matter—both of whom acknowledge the existence of critical economic power in the hands of fewer than three hundred corporations—depend on the nebulous or semimagical mechanisms of public opinion, self-responsibility among managers, and built-in competition that "fortunately" prevents oligopoly from becoming monopoly by creating new, although less substantial, centers of economic power (labor unions, consumers associations, etc.).

The pluralist argument espousing the need for gradual change is inadequate also, in the sense that it mistakenly presumes the instruments of gradualism to be readily available to those groups that are dispossessed in society. This obviously is not the case in the southern states where Negroes have no real place in the judicial, economic, and political systems—usually seen as the three main arenas through which peaceful change proceeds. The tools of gradualism are missing just as substantially, if less blatantly, throughout much of the North, where legislatures and city machines are built on widespread human denial. Can we be sure that a transition—specifically, actual public control of the economy—would proceed all the way by a gradual series of peacefully accepted reforms?

Beyond this, pluralist ideologues often discount the psychological sense of personal ineffectiveness that seems to make change difficult to create even where the formal tools of change are apparently present. Mills was extremely bitter toward this point of view, equating it with socialist realism because of its engulfing "long term historical optimism about the system as a whole and the goals proclaimed by its leaders." ("Let the old women complain wisely about the end of ideology," he declared also.)

Mills said, correctly, that the end-of-ideology perspective was itself an ideology, one supportive of American institutions. That

Mills was right in seeing the prematurity of this judgment is one of the conclusions one must draw from an examination of the deep-seated racial and economic tensions still remaining in the 1960s. The fashionable equation of ideology with destructive illusion (Stalinism) and the argument that modern complexity has rendered outmoded ideological forms of thought are both oversimplifications based on the experience of Russia and on radical disillusionment. They deny what seems desperately needed: a way to deal comprehensively with events—without oversimplification, to be sure, but also without trivializing them. Is it not realistic to take into account the dangers of excessive hope, and the need for greater intellectual sophistication, and then proceed from there to the development of an ideological mode of thought—one that constantly tries to evaluate trends as they affect or are affected by the life of the individual, with an eye to the possibilities for desirable change? It is true that the tradition of Marxism is in desperate need of renovation, but this should be seen as a call to scholarly and political work—as Mills quite properly saw it—and not as "Taps" for social theory and idealism. Mills, it should be remembered, faced an end of ideology, too, but he blamed the end on new developments in technology and social control that had undercut the revolutionary potential of specific classes and groups. The liberal end-of-ideologists misdirected the blame by embracing the new corporate society and dismissing ideological efforts to grasp its complexity.

Perhaps this narrowing of vision has been the main symptom of the demise of liberalism into a defensive and opportunistic stance toward threats and problems as they arise. It seemed to Mills that it was left as a set of grand but ambiguous ideals, barren of images of what is decisive to do or how things might be changed. The damning paradox was that liberalism covets "the open mind" as a property uniquely its own among political philosophies, but liberalism cringes, almost by definition, from being open to radical proposals. To be truly open requires that the liberal span a great contradiction: how to treat all ideals with equal inquisitiveness when some of them ask that he disrupt the well-integrated character of his life. Liberalism, in Mills's time, was anesthetized.

Mills's social theory, however, could not disclose the social, political, and technological crises that characterize the new era; hence, he did not sense the opportunity for new politics, of a neoliberal or even radical sort. Even his unfinished writings, published posthumously, made only brief mention of the student sit-in movements. His profound disgust with the self-serving liberal and Marxian establishments left Mills as a radical nomad, politically and ideologically. It was not until the last two years of his life that he began to find comrades, and even then, outside the United States. He found social thought similar to his own in Europe, among the young leftist and religious intellectuals of the post-Stalin period; and the young revolutionaries of the third world, he came to believe, reflected the greatest chance for "new beginnings," for a break with the binding control systems of the industrialized nations. He used the term "the New Left" to project this new tendency and furiously began work on an opus by that name. According to Irving L. Horowitz, Mills's literary executive, *The New Left* was to be nothing less than "an architectonic of socialism as a political ideology, as an ethic and as an institutional agency for social change."

This cosmic purpose was logically necessary if the major political ideologies were in need of revision, as Mills thought they were. The New Left would have to be a social force representing the revolutionary motor of world history. In *The Marxists,* he announced his intention dramatically: "It is not the purpose of this book to work out a political philosophy adequate to the world era which we now enter. But it is my hope that it will serve my readers, and myself, as an *introduction* to nothing less than just such an effort."

The task of political philosophy for Mills, was to explain society, point up ideals, and specify the forces capable of realizing them (by this definition, he equated philosophy with what others would call ideology). In other unfinished notes he wrote:

We have not known how serious the crisis of political philosophy is because it has not been really felt as a crisis in the advanced capitalist world. For due to a number of geographical accidents and historical good fortune, not to mention exploitative relations with less developed countries, especially in Latin America, the US has not experienced any crisis in political philosophy. Liberalism has been good enough. But if it is good enough to outcompete communism inside the United States, and most of Western Europe, that is not where the competition is going on. The hysteric about *that* rather pitiful competition, and about the long-distance interchanges between the United States and the Soviet Union have obscured from us the real locale of a competition.... That locale is to our South and to our East, in Latin America, Asia and Africa. It is true that we now begin to see the results of the crisis of our political philosophy. And if we value, and say we do, the ideals of Western Civilization, then we must see that it is a crisis not only of one political philosophy but of political philosophy itself.

Mills saw a need for intellectuals in the Western industrial countries to "break loose" and deal with this crisis of philosophy. He identified with few New Left currents in Europe who faced circumstances somewhat similar to his own: radicals without faith in the degenerated parties and classes that traditionally formed the agency of change. The European New Left was, and is, a reflection of general and moral and intellectual revulsion at the conditions of their generation: the thermonuclear technology, official hypocrisy, and national apathy. These circumstances led many young intellectuals into the ambiguous terrain between Marxism and existentialism. Without confidence in the built-in progressive character of the former, the underlying despair of the latter seemed in harmony with the mood of protest. This was, in essence, the tension between freedom and historical necessity that Mills attributed to the plain Marxists. It was a protest orientation, however, without suitable notice of strategy and goal. As one German participant argues:

Many still have not overcome their resentment to professional politics which they correctly correlate with the apathy of the masses. Others have gained strong influence in political parties.... Others, again, at odds with the socialist parties, try to revive the bureaucratized labor unions.... Some, like the Japanese and American students, are largely on their own and little related to other organizations.

Being in its beginnings, the New Left cannot be expected to have an elaborated program and theoretical homogeneity. This weakness is also its strength: the intellectual openness, its range from the liberal center to the socialist left, including all denominations.

This "new revisionism," to Mills a hopeful sign, appeared generally across Europe in the mid-1950s. In Eastern Europe, after the death of Stalin and more so after the denunciations at the Twentieth Party Congress in 1956, young socialists revolted. In East Germany, the call for a humanist Marxism was generated by intellectuals around Wolfgang Harich, who questioned the relevance of Marxist economics to current problems and demanded a loosening of the party dictatorship and a free discussion of theoretical and moral problems. As in East Germany, Czech intellectuals petitioned the party for a special congress to discuss the meaning of the new anti-Stalinist policies. In Hungary, young intellectuals created the Petofi Circle as a center for ideological discussion. In Poland, students turned their newspaper, *Po Prostu,* under the editorship of the "plain Marxist" Leszek Kolakowski, into a national journal for the discussion of reforms.

In the Soviet Union, too, an intellectual protest was stirring. Lewis Feuer and others have pointed out that the publication in Russia of Marx's 1844 *Economic and Philosophic Manuscripts* was a political, not an intellectual, decision, an accommodating response to the new currents of enthusiasm for moral discussion inside the Soviet Union.

In the meantime, a revival of Marxist thought was under way outside the communist countries. In France, Catholic theologians and secular radicals united in the reconstruction of Marxism as a consistent humanism; numerous works—by Sartre, Calvez, and Goldmann, especially—are the products of this search for the link between the existential and the Marxian traditions.

A similar concern evolved in West Germany where Protestant theologians—in particular, Irving Fetscher and the late Erwin Metzke—turned out three volumes of *Marximus-Studien* by the late 1950s. In Italy, the journal *Ragionmenti* was born in 1955 as a relation of the French *Arguments,* both forums for the new Marxists.

Perhaps Mills most identified with the British New Left, a circle of intellectuals, some new to politics, some ex-communists and Trotskyists, who shared a moral anxiety about nuclear weapons, Hungary, and Suez. In the later 1950s and 1960s they practiced what Mills demanded of intellectuals, by publishing *Conviction* and *Out of Apathy,* collections of New Left essays. In their work can be found an interest in personal codes as well as historical processes; in a fraternal society as well as public ownership; in richness of culture as well as rationality of economy; in existential revolt as well as strategic designs. It was to them, in 1960, that Mills addressed his "Letter to the New Left." It was in this essay that he first mightily stressed the problem of the agencies of change; but he was quite vague about the character of the New Left that he envisioned, except to say it was young, morally humanistic, intellectual, and action oriented. In the Cuba book, he added more specific characteristics: freedom from the bitter disillusion and defeat of the earlier leftist battles. The socialist "revolution" was broken and defeated all over Europe, accommodated to capitalism, turned to bureaucratic and cold war purposes. The working classes were beginning the ascent to affluence—at least the status of affluence—characteristic of America. Therefore, it was that Mills turned to the hungry-nation bloc, rather than Europe, as the central location of political revolt in the coming period. If the struggle between rich and poor, privileged and manipulated, could not be generated *within* the industrial countries, then perhaps it could be *internationalized.*

The New Left of those lands was even freer of the old political struggles than the New Left in Europe; their living situation was explosively revolutionary, and, above all, they had political commitment and moral hope. They were "new men" who could make a "new beginning" at "new kinds of revolution" because they lived in "new kinds of social structure having new kinds of ideologies and innovative forms."

Though Mills never put it this way, he seemed to believe that these revolutionaries could skip the usual stages of revolution, (1) the revolution against colonialism and (2) the revolution for cultural or qualitative freedom with a planned economy. "So it is," spoke the Cuban revolutionary in *Listen, Yankee,*

> we think that [only] in a revolutionary epoch intellectuals can do their real work and it is only by intellectual work that revolutions can be truly successful.... We'd like to say too that we don't think anybody in the world has really solved the problem of establishing the best chances for art and literature and culture in general.
>
> On the one hand, there's your capitalist way of doing it. It's a commercial establishment.... On the other hand, there's the Soviet way—state or party control of all cultural activity.... We aim to do better. We want our new cultural establishment to be part of our revolution, and so, like the revolution itself, we want them to be free and useful and beautiful and fluent.

And so, at the time of his death, Mills was ready to go forward with the reconstruction of political philosophy and a "world sociology" inclusive of all the elements of the third world. He still could not come up with a real expectation for a movement in America, except of a significant protest variety. The depths of his mood were revealed in *Listen, Yankee.*

> We Cuban revolutionaries don't really know just exactly *how* you could go about this transforming of Yankee imperialism. For us, with our problems, it was simple: In Cuba we had to take to our "Rocky Mountains"—you couldn't do that, could you? Not yet, we suppose. We're joking—we suppose. But if in ten years, if in

five years, if things go as we think they might inside your country, if it comes to that, then know this, Yankee: some of us will be with you. God almighty, those are great mountains!

What Mills overlooked was the underdevelopment within the United States as well as the third world. The contradictions between underdevelopment and potential abundance, between growing social protest and degenerate institutions, are bringing political ferment back to the Untied States. The immediate force for change is the Negro rights movement, but in its accomplishment of desegregation, it is elevating the larger problem of poverty to national prominence. This is the consequence of *decisions—power elite decisions*—made in the years Mills inherited. The decision to fix attention on foreign enemies; to use public resources for primarily military purposes; to permit the petty right in Congress and regions such as the South and the Midwest to rampage against national laws, ideals, and traditions; to rely on expansion, private capital, and militarism to generate a commonwealth.

Perhaps these decisions have resulted in qualitative changes in productive and military systems, bringing a new era—with the power elite on the defensive but not defeated. In any case, the era would be new for Mills in four decisive ways: the nation is waking up to domestic and moral issues; the political spectrum subtly is beginning to widen; the liberal establishment of the postwar years is being unsettled and challenged; an American New Left is being created. Had he lived, the nomad would have found comrades in the land.

The Kennedy administration began with the usual attention to the international scene—Cuba, Laos, Vietnam, Berlin, and so forth—but within two years became deeply occupied with the national life, especially because of the civil rights crisis of 1963. Since Kennedy's death (and didn't millions of Americans associate that tragedy, directly or indirectly, with some trouble deep in the American soul?), the new president repeatedly is taken up with national problems. This is so, even though the international

crisis—particularly in the underdeveloped areas—has, if anything, enlarged in the last year. Johnson's first State of the Union
message was, in terms of time allocation, a reverse of the Kennedy
stress on global concerns. Johnson spoke most of all to the need
for a tax cut and a civil rights bill, barely at all about the cold
war. If it is conceded that politicians reflect their context, then
the pattern is clear: many Americans are demanding that their
interests come before traditionally defined cold war interests.

In the face of these demands, some leaders have reacted with
statesmanlike grace. An example is Senator William J. Fulbright,
who said in a little-reported speech in spring 1964:

> Of all the changes wrought in American life by the cold war, the
> most important by far, in my opinion, has been the massive diver-
> sion of energy and resources from the creative pursuits of civilized
> society to the conduct of a costly and interminable struggle for
> world power. The result has been accumulating neglect of those
> things which bring happiness and beauty and fulfillment into
> our lives.... The cold war has diverted us from problems both
> quantitative and qualitative. The quantitative problem is essen-
> tially to devise ways of elevating the one-fifth of our people who
> live in poverty to the level of the four-fifths who live in greater
> material abundance than any other society in human history.
> While the attention and energy of our public policy have been
> focused through these postwar years of crises in Berlin and Cuba
> and the Far East, America has been more and more taking on the
> physical appearance and the cultural atmosphere of a honkytonk
> of continental proportions.

Others are reacting from more dubious intentions: everywhere
is found the practice of aggressive tokenism, the administrative
adjustment to the new era. There is a civil rights bill meant to
"take the conflict out of the streets" but that is so dependent on
the injunctive process and state courts that it will be only margin-
ally effective. There is a tax cut meant to increase employment but
inadequate to offset the combination of population and automation crises. There is a war on poverty with an annual budget less

than the *weekly* allocation for defense. And these adjustments are not confined merely to the domestic sphere: the American-Soviet détente itself partially represents a response to insurgency within the two superstates. The point is not simply that response is inadequate to the needs, however, but that it actually is a *response—a motion extracted from the elites by dissatisfied people.* A political time, of unknown scope and duration, is here again. It is a time of opening discussion, as the new and popular debates about poverty, automation, youth and delinquency, racial integration, and other issues testify. For the first time in years, many people will listen to the radical intellectual, if he still has the mind and voice. Such a climate did not exist or was only beginning, just two years ago at the time of Mills's death.

The "American consensus" is proving artificial. It is by no means a class struggle that is shattering the consensus, however. Presently the cause is the recurring flare and threat of disorder, and it is more over racial, status, and sectional differences than over class issues, though class issues are latent.

A massive reactionary movement, with the estimated sympathy of twenty to thirty million Americans, is the first and perhaps largest "dissident" force. The evidence is that the right wing is composed of provincial, religiously fundamentalist, and rural elements; insecure lower- and lower-middle-class urban elements; many corporation personnel in the West and South; and, most dangerously, many military leaders, especially in the air force and Strategic Air Command. These represent the forces that actually stand to lose important values in the transformation toward the new-era policies of détente, civil rights, and expanded liberal welfare programs. At present they work "within the system," for example, through local Republican organizations, school boards, and so forth, but while developing an "independent base" of followers. The question of whether they will bring into a more extreme counterrevolution, and who their allies will be at that point, is profoundly important—and impossible to gauge with available predictive measures. No one knows whether a military-inspired coup or preventive war is in the works, and there is no certain, empirical way to find out. Nor does anyone know under what combination of present and new conditions the American Right would be able to recruit more broadly and from what occupational groups and strata. For instance, pressures for northern school desegregation suddenly aroused militant opposition from *new* groups of middle class "inactionaries." One can only guess, for now, that the significant public support for the nuclear test ban, the civil rights bill, and the rejection of the organized right wing by most sizeable conservative magazines and organizations are signs that the Right is neither coming to power nor likely to force American politics to a greater stalemate between the old and new eras. The Barry Goldwater campaign, from this perspective, is not a qualitatively new advance for the American Right. In the first place, Goldwater himself shows signs of moving toward the center; in the second place, political polls indicate that Johnson will win by a larger majority than any president since Roosevelt in 1936. Of course, the constitutional defeat of the reactionaries might further encourage a militarist and violent tactic on their part.

There is a second important extremist movement in the United States, a radical one based on denial of racial and social opportunity. Its composition is almost entirely Negro, including frustrated individuals of both middle- and lower-class status of all ages and geographic areas. Some but not most of these persons are black Muslims; the rest either are involved in "conventional" civil rights activity or are quietly smoldering "private citizens," often armed. Their power does not include the ability to make world war or to attempt seizing the reins of government. Rather, it lies in the ability to paralyze key sectors of America, especially urban areas, through direct violent or nonviolent action. They have a lucid message—Freedom Now—but as yet no consensus on a political program of legislative proposals. What effect, direct and indirect, they will have on the political process is not possible to measure, though so far they seem to extract adjustive, administrative, and sometimes authoritarian responses.

These extremes are not *classes,* though they tend to represent segments of classes (and that is part of their threat to the elites).

They represent a threat to class stability, moreover, which is difficult to manage. Since their needs, whether expressed or objective ones, seem incompatible with the existing reward system, they are threat to the ideology and practice of consensus. That their needs are insoluble without reforms of a drastic sort makes the consensus tactic eventually inapplicable, and therefore the problem mounts so long as it is used.

In this spiral of tension, there may or may not be a breaking point, at which segments of the middle and upper classes, crying, "Do something," would bring on an *explicitly* authoritarian national system. Assuming this does not happen, the stalemate system is with us for the time being—with the ascendant corporation nagging by the irrationality of the lingering market, with opulence breeding at the top and neglect proceeding at the bottom, with anxiety and even terror growing in the middle classes, frustration and resentment in the lower. Anything can happen. Much will depend on the role of the adjustive and adjusting elites: they were used to their role in the postwar consensus, but now are vacillating, uncertain, about their moves in the new situation.

Among these center elements is organized liberalism, the establishment so greatly responsible for the ideology of the end-of-ideology. To some major extent, the stability of any political bloc depends on long-term constituent satisfaction, and it is here that liberalism of the postwar variety is today being challenged from two directions. The first challenge is from many of the direct and declared constituents: the unionized labor force, the Negroes, Puerto Ricans, Mexicans, and Indians; the small farmers; the organized senior citizens; the middle-class and professional people who are concerned with issues of housing and welfare, war and peace, and racial equality. The neglected social and priorities of the cold war years are the cause of this hunger for reform. The number of contracts rejected by union locals has risen rapidly to its postwar high; ADA conventions are split over questions of racial, economic, and nuclear policy. The NAACP, Urban League, and CORE are ridden with strife over the degree of militance and content of program, and they are challenged to greater lengths of effort by radicals in the Student Nonviolent Coordinating Committee and other organizations. In the meantime, *The Nation, The New Republic, The Progressive,* and other magazines from the reform tradition are sprinkled with articles attacking liberalism's "failure of nerve."

The second "constituency" of liberalism has been made up of all the out-groups whose presence is suddenly being felt, or threatening to be felt, in the political process. These primarily are the poorest poor—rural and slum Negroes, the long-term unemployed Appalachian miners and migrant laborers, and so forth. They represent an "available constituency"—one that would increase liberal power if they were politically registered and active.

This would seem a fine opportunity for the liberal-left, but it is not clear that the liberal-left has the will, vision, and program to satisfy these various groups. Even to *keep* its disaffected constituency, quite apart from recruiting a new base, will require established liberal leaders to endanger their niches within the American hierarchy, take a risk instead of following power. Labor might have to threaten politically not to support Democratic Party candidates; labor and civil rights organizations would have to build a political program linking the questions of unemployment, racism, overcommitment to the defense sector, and the conservative Congress. Not only might this lead to short- and long-term discourtesies for the rest of the Democratic Party, but it would also open up major leadership struggles in the liberal community—something that has not often occurred in organized labor, for instance, since the 1940s. This, of course, is already occurring in some areas and is incipient in others. In brief, liberalism now is in the process of realigning its internal structure and outer limits.

The outcome of this situation is unclear, but it will be in large measure shaped by two factors. The first is that even a moderate solution to the problem of poverty, structural unemployment, and discrimination will require very soon an end to the irrational conservative fear of government in the economy. This means a new and "modernized" Congress capable of elaborating the liberal vision of the corporate state. It is clear that the Kennedy and even the Johnson administrations desire congressional reform more than any presidents since Roosevelt defeated Landon in 1936. It is also clear that liberal forces are beginning to direct their most serious attention to a strengthened coalition for a new Congress, as the only alternative to "disorder." Whether this country, and specifically the corporate elite, will accept the "liberal solution" is an unsettled question. The crisis of the 1930s was visible and pressing; this one is relatively invisible and dissonant to the comfortable patterns of the business community. The crisis of the 1930s emerged squarely as an economic one; this crisis, through profoundly economic in character, emerged as a racial and regional one. If, therefore, support cannot be gathered to create a new Congress, then a deeper crisis will develop, and with it perhaps new leaders and programs.

The other fact shaping the future of liberalism is the emergence already of a new stratum of insurgent, radical leadership since the late 1950s. This group requires special attention; it is a developing new American Left and most certainly would have given Mills a company with which to share his feelings, fears, and creative power. The New Left is not a party, a group, or a movement, though it is probably all of these in process. In the upheaval of new protest movements, and in the vacuum created by the liberal default, there is developing a new kind of radicalism. Its immediate sources are the civil rights movement, unemployment councils, student and some faculty groups, the militant sectors of the industrial union organizations, the peace movement, and the literary and cultural communities. It is just a feeling, but would Mills not "document" this New Left in that distant, but personally revealing, monologue form he used brilliantly? Perhaps this is how he would have put it:

> Most of us are from the middle classes, but increasingly some of us are from the working class, and, anyway, all of us are identified with the poorest—and not in some sentimental but in a

serious, pretty angry way. What experience we have is our own, not vicarious or inherited. The little there is of it includes some important and lasting facts: those of brutality, racism, and economic savagery toward people we know, and people we are; those of the public drift and private malaise of people who are doing well financially; those established facts that suppress and drain the heart of protest. Only a few of us come from families of the Left; and they had to go through a hell all of their own to find an independent place to stand. For the rest of us, our radicalism is rooted in, and comes out of—both at once—the experience of living in a society so deadened that it may be forever unaware of its own selfish and craven way of life, not to speak of the way of life it *could* lead. We are mostly innocent of the history of the Left, and many of us feel glad of it, because the Left is associated with sectarianism, defeat and musty battles, and a lot of clichés. That does not mean we have a patronizing attitude to the Left, nor that we are born new in history; the history of the Left especially is replete with tragedies and beauties that partially form our circumstances, for better and for worse. It does mean, though, that we are a new generation, in need of the freedom to work out our own relationship to this society in its post–cold war, postscarcity stage.

We don't believe in any science of strategy and tactics. We are pretty practical people, concerned with direct action that can immediately make some change and create new openings. Direct action is the new ingredient: strikes and electoral action and lobbying have to be redefined in terms of their current suitability, and brought into a context of direct action as techniques.

We know the importance of talking about and organizing around issues that are at one and the same time meaningful to people and radical. Issues such as unemployment, useless and diversionary work, civil rights, the schools our kids attend, which make up the issue of everyday life while also telling us clearly what we are, what we could be, and what prevents the realization of what we could be. We think economic problems are the fundamental ones that connect most of the others, but we don't neglect the cultural and personal problems that can't be postponed, especially not in a society as affected by communications as this one. We figure it will take a long time, and much experimental work, before we come to reach all the people the movement needs to take power—which is one of the things we are seeking.

Note

1. Writing in a somewhat calmer period a few years later, anti-communist socialists Howe and Coser, in their *History of American Communism,* expressed grave worries about the fights of the 1940s: "Granting the desirability of eliminating communist influence from the trade union movement, one might still have argued that the mass expulsions not only were a poor way for achieving this end but constituted a threat to democratic values and procedures.... But in the atmosphere of 1949 and 1950 not many people troubled to reflect on such problems."

Notes, Methodology, Bibliography

Thisisthefirstdraftofanintellectualbiographyand
a reflective essay. It tries to explain, analyze, and chart the ideas
of C. Wright Mills as they developed over a twenty-five-year period. It also attempts to relate these writings meaningfully in the
circumstances of the times and thus suggest a partial framework
for viewing American history since the 1930s.

The intellectual problems and choices were quite difficult.
Perhaps they can be understood by pointing out the real gaps I
feel in this analysis in its present stage of formulation. Some of
these gaps I personally intend to work at filling, and, needless to
say, success in this effort will require the work of many others.

First, there is a need for a complete biography of Mills. Some
of the transitions in his work cannot satisfactorily be explained
without incorporating material about Mills the human being—for example, the differences between his books on labor
and the Puerto Ricans, the series of tracts published in the late
1950s, or his emergent interest in the third world. Moreover, his
turbulent associations with liberals and the Left, sociologists and
academia, editors and other writers, would provide an enriching
view of the politics and sociology of the 1940s and 1950s. Finally,
certain characteristics of his life and personality—his bombast,
amazing energy, variety of talents, relations with women, other

193

friendships, strained connections with most political intellectuals, personal worries, heart attacks—all suggest a historically important biography. His was an existential personality, embodying
some of the master problems of the times—the struggle of the
radical intellect against alienation and isolation; the struggle of
humanist social theory against the segmentation of knowledge
and the larger cleavage of fact from value; the struggle for moral-
ity amid moral breakdown.

Second, there is a need to place Mills in a more thorough and
historical framework of modern political and social thought.
What were his major contributions to this tradition? What previous modes of thought, or individual theorists, were the key
sources of his orientation? Some rough efforts have been made
to tie Mills to Marx, Veblen, Weber, Mannheim, Pareto, Mosca,
and others, but as yet there has been no thorough interpretation
of his significance in the history of ideas. There has been some
effort, but certainly not enough, to locate Mills in the radical
traditions of America and Europe. The need to do this work is
especially important for those trying to define the significance of
their own political and intellectual work, for it is doubtful that
one can simply leap over Mills instead of using and building on
the materials he left behind. This need is just as great for the conservative as for the radical: Mills's statements were too formidable
to be ignored by anyone with a historical consciousness.

Third, there is need for more empirical work on his propo-
sitions. Given his immense descriptive talents, it is somewhat
unfortunate that Mills never focused his full powers on a mi-
crocosmic case or problem (e.g., the legitimation of the labor
movement in the 1930s; the biography of James Forrestal or
Joseph McCarthy; the reconversion controversy of the mid-1940s;
the decisions to bomb Hiroshima, Nagasaki, and Dresden).
This "neglect" permitted severe criticism of his method and an
escape from facing his conclusions. Moreover, to many it gave
his work an irrelevant and remote character because he too
summarily dismissed the events that ordinarily glut the media
and conversation. Intellectuals with Mills's orientation have not

sufficiently supplemented his work with close-up studies. Where is a contemporary book to compare with *Middletown in Transition*? Where is there systematic, organized radical inquiry into the operations of American society? With a few exceptions, such as Engler's *The Politics of Oil,* most radical inquiry is taking place *outside* the university community, among "new muckrakers" such as Cook, Harrington, Mitford, and Nossiter.

However, it is not merely a *lack* of research in these areas that presents a problem. The research itself is problematic, especially because of the difficulty in examining "latent" or "underlying" phenomena (e.g., the unused social resources, the potential of specific groups for different modes of behavior, the "conditions" under which consciousness is changed, the durability of common elite interests, etc.). Much of Mills's argument rested on his charge that the intellectuals were studying close-up events at the expense of greater, determining ones.

> One continual weakness of American social science, since it became ever so empirical, has been its assumption that a mere enumeration of a plurality of causes is the wise and scientific way of going about understanding modern society. Of course, it is nothing of the sort: it is a paste-pot eclecticism which avoids the real task of social analysis: that task is to go beyond a mere enumeration of all the facts that might conceivably be involved and weigh each of them in such a way as to understand how they fit together, how they form a model of what it is you are trying to understand.

There are complex empirical ways to plot an "unspoken consensus" (e.g., by analyzing the contested and uncontested premises in a series of decisions), to hypothesize about available resources, to infer future from past behavior; but they indeed are rough and aggregate. Hence, Mills often was charged with confusing power-potential with power-use. I have no special answer to such a problem, but at least it seems incumbent on social scientists to put as much ingenuity into the investigation of these broad questions as into their studies of "the middle levels."

Even were these needs met to a greater extent than at present, there would be a further, social obstacle. That is the existence, in a supposedly democratic society, of private control over the means of investigation and exposure. American democracy is turning into little more than the collusion and collision of secret bureaucracies. The manipulation of fact is becoming pervasive and is generally seen as legitimate. In the economic sphere, as Kolko most recently pointed out, there are numerous "barriers of deception and silence" and "ingenious forms of income" separating the investigator from the truth. The clear fact is that the controllers of privately incorporated wealth are required to supply the public with only minimal amounts of information, and even this information is often found to be spurious. In the military sphere, the "classified" mantle extends over the entire decision-making and planning process. More recently, the political institutions have increased their forms of secrecy. This has taken place through the elaboration of new executive bureaucracies outside the traditional representative ones. Increasingly, the executive has expropriated the right to regulate economic development, foreign trade, and military actions. This has been accompanied by improved and enlarged kinds of manipulation of news and information. Examples of this are abundant. When caught lying about the U-2 by Khrushchev in 1958, Eisenhower called his lie of the previous day a "routine covering statement." This process was to become much more routinized under the Kennedy administration.

Some might argue that a degree of secrecy is inevitably part of bureaucratic organization, that "direct democracy" is an impossibility on the modern scene. This interpretation, however, neglects the fact that no one has *tried* to make information a public property in the United States. The more accurate point is that information is a form of private property produced and distributed by the few. No amount of comparison between the United States and the Soviet Union in this respect is to the point. Totalitarianism does not require overt dictatorship and terror; it only requires hegemony over the establishment of accepted fact.

Whether we are still approaching that situation in the United States, or whether we are already past it, are questions for which there are no accessible answers.

Take one example directly from Mills's own research. He attempted with great difficulty to find valued information about the three most recent generations of the very rich (those who came to maturity in the 1890s, those of the mid-1920s, and those of midcentury). First, he availed himself of all biographical works, such as those of Gustavus Myers, Ferdinard Lundberg, and Frederick Lewis Allen. Second, he relied on the two partial revelations of wealth that have appeared in this century. The first was in 1924–1925 when a temporary law "allowed the release of information on the size of income tax payments for 1923 and 1924. Journalists were admitted to various offices of the Bureau of Internal Revenue and there copied names with the taxes paid by each." The release of these data was "administratively sloppy." Moreover, it is difficult to calculate gross wealth from income tax returns. Mills had to make complicated and tenuous assumptions: for instance, that average taxes took about 40 percent of real income and that about one-third of most entire fortunes at the time were in taxable sources.

The second revelation of income came with the Temporary National Economic Committee Reports of the late 1930s. These gave the twenty largest stockholders of record in each of the two hundred largest nonfinancial corporations, along with the stockholdings of the directors and officers of these corporations, as of 1937 or 1938. The list was incomplete, said Mills, because it did not cover "money held in government or local bonds, in real estate or financial houses. Moreover in a number of instances ownership even of industrial corporations is disguised by the practice of recording the ownership of a block of stock under various investment houses which do not divulge the names of the actual owners."

Mills also traced through obituaries to find where the fortunes went, especially looking for settlements involving more than $30 million.

Finally, he received spotty information from federal agencies, magazines, foundations, investment houses, and individuals. The result of the long search was striking: "Of the 371 names, I was unable to find, from a search of bibliographical sources, the books mentioned above and newspaper files, any information about the life of 69 of them." One-fifth of the richest people to live during the twentieth century are veiled in complete anonymity.

Due largely to the need for rapid editing and stenciling, there are no footnotes attached to this essay in its present form. They will be incorporated, however, in a later version. Until then, those who would appreciate specific sources may write me for them, care of the Center for Research on Conflict Resolution, University of Michigan. The general sources used are as follows:

A nearly complete bibliography of Mills's writings is available in *Power, Politics and People* (Horowitz, ed.). The works I have found most important are, in the order of their publication, "A Sociological Account of Pragmatism" (unpublished Ph.D. diss., University of Wisconsin, 1942); *From Max Weber: Essays in Sociology,* ed. with Hans Gerth (New York: Oxford University Press, 1946); *The New Men of Power* (New York: Harcourt, Brace, 1948); *The Puerto Rican Journey: New York's Newest Migrants,* with Clarence Senior and Rose K. Goldsen (New York: Oxford University Press, 1950); *White Collar: The American Middle Classes* (New York: Oxford University Press, 1951); *Character and Social Structure,* with Hans Gerth (New York: Harcourt, Brace, 1953); *The Power Elite* (New York: Oxford University Press, 1956); *The Causes of World War Three* (New York: Simon & Schuster, 1958); *The Sociological Imagination* (New York: Oxford University Press, 1959); *Listen, Yankee: The Revolution in Cuba* (New York: McGraw-Hill, 1960); *Images of Man: The Classic Tradition in Sociological Thinking* (New York: Braziller, 1960); *The Marxists* (New York: Dell, 1962); *Power, Politics and People: The Collected Essays of C. Wright Mills,* ed. Irving L. Horowitz (New York: Oxford University Press, 1963).

Horowitz also compiled a very nice bibliography and mono-graphs, essays, and reviews of Mills's work. The following is a shorter list, including a few selections not in Horowitz's bibliography, of diverse, important viewpoints. First, relevant books, monographs and essays: Aptheker, Herbert, *The World of C. Wright Mills* (New York: Marzani & Munsell, 1960); Bell, Daniel, "The Power Elite Reconsidered," *American Journal of Sociology* 64, no. 3 (1958): 238–50; Bell, Daniel, "Is There a Ruling Class in America?" in *The End of Ideology* (Glencoe, Ill.: Free Press, 1960); Dahrendorf, Ralf, "C. Wright Mills," *Kölner Zeitschrift für Soziologie und Sozial-psychologie* 14, no. 3: 603–5; Dahl, Robert, "Critique of the Ruling Class Model," *American Political Science Review* 52, no. 2 (June 1958): 463–70; Davis, Arthur, "Sociology without Clothes," *Monthly Review* (November 1959): 256–63; Feuer, Lewis, "A Symposium on C. Wright Mills' *The Sociological Imagination*," *Berkeley Journal of Sociology* 5, no. 1 (Fall 1959): 122–23; Gerth, Hans, "C. Wright Mills, 1916–1962," *Studies on the Left* 2, no. 3 (1962): 711; Kaufman, Arnold, "The Irresponsibility of American Social Scientists," *Inquiry: An Interdisciplinary Journal of Philosophy and the Social Sciences* 2 (1960): 102–17; Meisel, James, *The Myth of the Ruling Class* (Ann Arbor: University of Michigan Press, 1962); Parsons, Talcott, "The Structure of Power in American Society," in *Structure and Process in Modern Societies* (Glencoe, Ill.: Free Press, 1960); Rosenberg, Bernard, and Watler, Eugene, "The Power Elite: Two Views," *Dissent* (Fall 1956): 390–98; Ross, Robert, "The Power and the Intellect: (unpublished honors thesis, University of Michigan, 1963); Lipset, Seymour, and Smelser, Neil, "Charge and Controversy in Recent American Sociology," *British Journal of Sociology* 19, no. 1 (March 1961): 41–51; Sweezy, Paul, "Power Elite or Ruling Class," *New Review* (September 1956): 133–39; Wolfe, Robert, "Intellectuals and Social Change," *Studies on the Left* 2, no. 3 (1962): 63–68.

Second, more specific reviews (with Mills's titles abbreviated): Berle, A., "Are the Blind Leading the Blind?" *New York Times Book Review* (April 22, 1956) (*PE*); Chase, Stuart, "Do Rich Folks,

Bosses and Warlords Run America?" *Harold Tribune Book Review* (July 1, 1956 (*PE*); Cochran, Bert, "C. Wright Mills' Anti-War Manifesto," *American Sociologist* (May 1959): 18–21 (*WWT*); Coser, Lewis, "The Uses of Sociology," *Partisan Review* 27, no. 1 (Winter 1960): 166–73 (*TSI*); Crossman, P. H. S., "Grooming for Power," *The New Statesmen* and *The Nation*; Engler, Robert, "Power without Accountability," *New Republic* (April 1956) (*PF*); Lynd, Robert S., "Power in the United States," *The Nation* 182, no. 19 (May 12, 1956): 408–11 (*PE*); Muste, A. J., and Howe, Irving, "C. Wright Mills' Program: Two Views," *Dissent* 6, no. 2 (Spring 1954): 189–96 (*WWT*); Rossi, Peter, "Review of *The Power Elite*," *American Journal of Sociology* 2 (September 1956) (*PE*); Schlesinger, Arthur, "This Isn't the Way," *New York Post*, December 7, 1958 (*WWT*); Shils, Edward, "Imaginary Sociology," *Encounter* (June 1960): 77–81.

I should like to acknowledge particular works by three other authors, besides Mills, that deeply influenced my own angle of vision. One is Herbert Marcuse: *Reason and Revolution* (Boston: Beacon, 1941), 60; *Soviet Marxism* (New York: Random House, 1958); *Eros and Civilization* (Boston: Beacon, 1960); *One-Dimensional Man* (Boston: Beacon, 1960). Another has been William Appleman Williams: *The Tragedy of American Diplomacy* (New York: World, 1959); *The Contours of American History* (New York: World, 1961). A third has been Raymond Williams: *Culture and Society* (London: Chatto & Windus, 1959); *Border Country* (London: Chatto & Windus, 1960); *The Long Revolution* (London: Chatto & Windus, 1961). Theirs has been an impact too powerful to merely recognize in footnotes.

The specific orientation of this essay stems from three previous essays that I helped to write. Two of them are official organizational documents of Students for a Democratic Society: "The Port Huron Statement" (1962) and "America in the New Era" (1963). The other, written with Richard Flacks, is *The New Possibilities for Peace* (Ann Arbor: Peace Research and Education

Project, Students for a Democratic Society, 1963), part of which appeared in *Liberation* (November 1963): 14–19.

In addition to many of the aforementioned books, there are many that confront the nature of contemporary society and the question of a postrevolutionary, or postideological, even postindustrial, epoch. Some of the most durable over the last three decades have been Arendt, Hannah, *The Origins of Totalitarianism* (New York: Harcourt, Brace, 1951); Bell, Daniel, *The End of Ideology* (Glencoe, Ill.: Free Press, 1960); Berle, Adolph (with Gardner C. Means), *The Modern Corporation and Private Property* (New York: Macmillan, 1932); Berle, Adolph, *The Twentieth Century Capitalist Revolution* (Garden City, N.Y.: Doubleday, 1954); Berle, Adolph, *Power without Property* (New York: Harcourt, Brace & World, 1959); Burnham, James, *The Managerial Revolution* (New York: Day, 1941); Carr, E. H., *The New Society* (Boston: Beacon, 1951); Dahrendorf, Ralf, *Class and Class Consciousness in Industrial Society* (London: Routledge & Kegan Paul, 1959); Durkheim, Emile, *The Division of Labor* (Glencoe: Free Press, 1947); Fromm, Erich, *Escape from Freedom* (New York: Rinehart, 1941); Galbraith, John, *American Capitalism* (New York: Houghton, Mifflin, 1952); Kafka, Franz, *The Castle* (New York: Knopf, 1930); Kahler, Erich, *Man the Measure* (New York: Pantheon, 1943); Lipset, Seymour, *Political Man* (Garden City: Anchor, 1959); Mannheim, Karl, *Ideology and Utopia* (New York: Harcourt, Brace, 1936); Mannheim, Karl, *Man and Society in an Age of Reconstruction* (New York: Harcourt, Brace, 1950); Mumford, Lewis, *The Condition of Man* (New York: Harcourt, Brace, 1944); Neumann, Franz, *Behemoth* (London: Gollancz, 1943); Riesman, David, *The Lonely Crowd* (New Haven, Conn.: Yale University Press, 1950); Whyte, William, *Is Anybody Listening?* (New York: Simon & Schuster, 1950).

The interpretation of the postwar "strategy of stabilization" rests on the previously cited works but specifically also on the following. The buildup of the military is studied in Catton, Bruce,

Warlords of Washington (New York: Harcourt, Brace, 1948); Coffin, Tristram, *The Passion of the Hawks* (New York: Macmillan, 1964, 1948); Cook, Fred, *The Warfare State* (New York: Macmillan, 1962); Craven, W. F., and Care, J. L., eds., *Men and Planes* (Chicago: University of Chicago Press, 1955); Fleming, D. F., *The Origins of the Cold War* (Garden City, N.Y.: Doubleday, 1961); Ickes, Harold, *The Secret Diaries of Harold Ickes* (New York: Simon & Schuster, 1954); Kennan, George, *Russia, the Atom and the West* (New York: Mentor, 1960); Leahy, William, *I Was There* (New York: McGraw–Hill, 1950); Millis, Walter, ed., *The Forrestal Diaries* (New York: Viking, 1951); Raymond, Jack, *Power at the Pentagon* (New York: Harper & Row, 1964); Rogow, Arnold, *James Forrestal: A Study of Personality, Politics and Policy* (New York: Macmillan, 1963); Stebbins, Richard, *The United States in World Affairs* (New York: Harper and the Council on Foreign Relations, 1956); Strauss, Lewis, *Men and Decisions* (Garden City, N.Y.: Doubleday, 1962).

Another thorough history is available from the army: Watson, Mark-Skinner, *The War Department, Vol. I: Chief of Staff, Pre-War Plans and Preparations* (Washington, D.C.: Historical Division of the Department of the Army, 1950); Matloff, Maurice, and Snell, Edwin, *The War Department, Vol. II: Strategic Planning for Coalition Warfare, 1941–1942* (Washington, D.C.: Office of the Chief of Military History, Department of the Army, 1953); Cline, R. S., *The War Department, Vol. III: Washington Command Post: The Operations Division* (Washington, D.C.: Office of the Chief of Military History, Department of the Army, 1954). Mills called these "the best sources on the details of the military ascendancy in the political realm just before and during World War II."

Other material on politics in the immediate postwar period that has been useful: Meyer, Karl, *Henry A. Wallace: Quixotic Crusade* (Syracuse, N.Y.: Syracuse University, 1960). Other information on the Marcantonio campaigns was received from individuals involved in different factions at the time. The first postwar slump is carefully analyzed in Lewis, Wilfred, *Federal Fiscal Policy in the*

Postwar Recessions (Washington, D.C.: Brookings Institution, 1962). Other information on income, corporate and personal savings, profit levels, and so forth, is from the U.S. Bureau of the Census, *Statistical Abstract of the United States, 1962* (Washington, D.C.: U.S. Government Printing Office, 1962).

With regard to the theoretical problems of defining *power, class, status elite,* and other basic terms, I utilized a number of standard works: Bendix, Reinhard, and Lipset, Seymour, *Class, Status, and Power* (Glencoe, Ill.: Free Press, 1953); *Social Mobility in Industrial Society* (Glencoe, Ill.: Free Press, 1959); Carr, E. H., *What Is History?* (New York: Knopf, 1961); Keller, Suzanne, *Beyond the Ruling Class: The Strategic Elites in Modern Society* (New York: Random House, 1963); Lassell, Harold, and Kaplan, A., *Power and Society* (New Haven, Conn.: Yale University Press, 1950); Lynd, Robert, *Knowledge for What?* (Princeton, N.J.: Princeton University Press, 1946); Merton, Robert, *Social Theory and Social Structure* (Glencoe, Ill.: Free Press, 1949); Mosca, Gaetano, *The Ruling Class* (New York: McGraw-Hill, 1939); Moore, Barrington, *Political Power and Social Theory* (Cambridge, Mass.: Harvard University Press, 1958); Neumann, Franz, "Approaches to the Study of Political Power," *Political Science Quarterly* 65: 161–80; Pareto, Vilfredo, *The Mind and Society,* ed. Arthur Livingston, trans. Livingston and A. Biongorno (New York: Harcourt, Brace, 1935); Parsons, Talcott, *Essays in Sociological Theory* (Glencoe, Ill.: Free Press, 1949); Parsons, Talcott, *The Social System* (Glencoe, Ill.: Free Press, 1951); Veblen, Thorstein, *The Theory of the Leisure Class* (New York: Macmillan, 1899).

The problem of power in the United States is faced with varying degrees of explicitness in almost all of the preceding works. However, there are other more specific books and articles that have been helpful.

More on the military: Hayden, Thomas, "The New Disarmament Mood," in *The Correspondent* (1964); Horowitz, Irving: *The War Game* (New York: Ballantine, 1962); Huntington, Samuel,

The Soldier and the State (Cambridge, Mass.: Harvard University Press, Belknap, 1957); "Power, Expertise and the Military Profession," *Daedelus* (Fall 1963): 785–808; Janowitz, Morris, "Military Elites and the Study of War," *Journal of Conflict Resolution* 1 (1957): 9–18; Janowitz, Morris, *Sociology and the Military Establishment* (New York: Russell Sage Foundation, 1959); Janowitz, Morris, *The Professional Soldier* (Glencoe, Ill.: Free Press, 1960); Lyons, Gene, "The Military Mind," *Bulletin of the Atomic Scientists* (November 1963): 19–22; Janowitz, Morris, and Masland, A., *Education and Military Leadership* (Princeton, N.J.: Princeton University Press, 1959); Meisel, James, *The Fall of the Republic* (Ann Arbor: University of Michigan Press, 1962); Meisel, James, "Leviathan's Progress," *Queen's Quarterly* 55, no. 4 (1948): 402–3; Meynard, Jean, "Les Militaries et la pouvoir," *Revue Française du Sociologies* (April–June 1961): 83–84; Perlo, Victor, *Militarism and Industry* (New York: International, 1963); Sapin, Burton, and Snyder, Richard, *The Role of the Military in American Foreign Policy* (Garden City, N.Y.: Doubleday, 1954); Swomley, John, *The Military Establishment* (Boston: Beacon, 1964); Vagts, Alfred, *The History of Militarism* (New York: Norton, 1937); Waskow, Arthur, *The Limits of Defense* (Garden City, N.Y.: Doubleday, 1962).

The analysis of the political sphere utilized the following: Burns, James McGregor, *Congress on Trial: The Legislative Process and the Administrative State* (New York: Harper, 1949); Burns, James McGregor, *The Deadlock of Democracy: The Four-Party System* (New York: Prentice Hall, 1963); Hacker, Andrew, "The Elected and the Appointed," *American Political Science Review* (September 1961); Hayden, Thomas, "The Power of the Dixiecrats," *New University Thought* (December 1963–January 1964): 6–16; Hayden, Thomas, and Feingold, Eugene, "What Happened to Democracy?" *New University Thought* (April–May 1964): 39–48; Lubell, Samuel, *The Future of American Politics* (Garden City, N.Y.: Anchor, 1952); Matthews, Donald, *US Senators and Their World* (Chapel Hill: University of North Carolina Press, 1960); Rosow, Jerome, *American Men in Government* (Washington, D.C.: Public Affairs Press, 1949).

The problem of economic power: Baran, Paul, *The Political Economy of Growth* (New York: Monthly Review, 1957); Baran, Paul, and Sweezy, Paul, "Monopoly Capital," *Monthly Review* (July–August 1962); Bazelton, David, *The Paper Economy* (New York: Random House, 1963); Brady, Robert, *Business as a System of Power* (New York: Columbia University Press, 1943); Cochran, Thomas, *The American Business System* (New York: Harper, 1957); Cochran, Thomas, and Miller, William: *The Age of Enterprise* (New York: Harper, 1942); Cosser, Paul, *State Capitalism in the Economy of the United States* (New York: Bookman, 1960); Elliot, Osgorn, *Men at the Top* (New York: Harper, 1956; Editors of *Fortune, The Executive Life* (Garden City, N.Y.: Doubleday, 1956); Galbraith, John, *The Affluent Society* (New York: Houghton Mifflin, 1958); Hansen, Alvin, *The American Economy* (New Y: McGraw-Hill, 1956); Hansen, Alvin, *Economic Issues of the Sixties* (New York: McGraw-Hill, 1964); Kolko, Gabriel, *Wealth and Power in America* (Boston: Praeger, 1962); Lampman, Robert, "Changes in the Share of Wealth Held by Top Wealth Holders, 1922–1956," *Review of Economics and Statistics* 41 (November 1959): 379–92; Lynch, David, *The Concentration of Economic Power* (New York: Columbia University Press, 1946); Miller, William, ed., *Men in Business* (New York: Harper, 1952); Newcomer, Mabel, *The Big Business Executive* (New York: Columbia University Press, 1955); Nossiter, Bernard, *The Mythmakers* (New York: Houghton Mifflin, 1964); Perlo, Victor, *The Empire of High Finance* (New York: International, 1957); Reagan, Michael, *The Managed Economy* (New York: Oxford University Press, 1963); Sutton, Francis, et al., *The American Business Creed* (Cambridge, Mass.: Harvard University Press, 1956); Taussig, F. W., and Joslyn, C. S., *American Business Leaders* (New York: Macmillan, 1932); Villarejo, Donald, "Stock Ownership and the Control of Corporations," *New University Thought* (Autumn 1961); Warner, Lloyd, and Abegglen, James, *Big Business Leaders in America* (New York: Harper, 1955).

Some general works dealing with the character of power in the United States: Dahl, Robert, *Who Governs?* (New Haven,

Conn.: Yale University Press, 1961); Engler, Robert, *The Politics of Oil* (New York: Macmillan, 1961); Horowitz, Irving, ed., *The New Sociology: Essays in Memory of C. Wright Mills* (New York: Oxford University Press, 1964); Hunter, Floyd, *Community Power Structure* (Chapel Hill: University of North Carolina Press, 1953); Hunter, Floyd, *Top Leadership USA* (Chapel Hill: University of North Carolina Press, 1959); Kornhauser, Arthur, ed., *Problems of Power in American Democracy* (Detroit: Wayne State University Press, 1957); Lynd, Robert and Helen, *Middletown in Transition* (New York: Harcourt, Brace, 1937); Polsby, Nelson, *Community Power and Political Theory* (New Haven, Conn.: Yale University Press, 1963).

A number of government publications on economic power were quite helpful: Federal Trade Commission, *Report of the Federal Trade Commission on Interlocking Directorates* (Washington, D.C.: U.S. Government Printing Office, 1951); National Resources Committee, *The Structure of the American Economy—Part I, Basic Characteristics* (Washington, D.C.: U.S. Government Printing Office, 1939); Temporary National Economic Committee, *Concentration and Composition of Individual Incomes, 1918–1937,* Monograph No. 4 (Washington, D.C.: U.S. Government Printing Office, 1940); Temporary National Economic Committee, *The Distribution of Ownership in the 200 Largest Nonfinancial Corporations,* Monograph No. 29 (Washington, D.C.: U.S. Government Printing Office, 1940); Temporary National Economic Committee, *Survey of Shareholdings in 1,710 Corporations with Securities Listed on a National Securities Exchange,* Monograph No. 30 (Washington, D.C.: U.S. Government Printing Office, 1941); U.S. House of Representatives, Committee on the Judiciary, *Hearings before the Subcommittee on the Study of Monopoly Power of the Committee on the Judiciary,* Eighty-second Congress, First Session, Serial No. 1, Part 2 (Washington, D.C.: U.S. Government Printing Office, 1951; U.S. House of Representatives, Select Committee on Small Business: *Interlocking Directorates and Officials of 135 Large Financial Companies of the US,* Eighty-fifth Congress, First Session (Washington, D.C.: U.S. Government Printing Office) 1957; U.S. House of Representatives, *Tax-Exempt Foundations and Charitable Trusts: Their Impact on Our Economy,* Chairman's Reports, Eighty-seventh Congress (Washington, D.C.: U.S. Government Printing Office, December 31, 1962) and Eighty-eighth Congress (Washington, D.C.: U.S. Government Printing Office, October 16, 1963); U.S. Senate, Committee on the Judiciary, *Bigness and the Concentration of Economic Power—A Case Study of General Motors Corporation,* Eighty-fourth Congress, Second Session (Washington, D.C.: U.S. Government Printing Office, 1956; U.S. Senate, Committee on the Judiciary, *Study of Administered Prices in the Steel Industry,* Eighty-fifth Congress, Second Session (Washington, D.C.: U.S. Government Printing Office, 1958); U.S. Senate, Committee on Finance, *Stock Options,* Hearings, Eighty-seventh Congress, First Session (Washington, D.C.: U.S. Government Printing Office, July 21–22, 1961).

Material on "mass society" and "class society": Bell, Daniel, ed., *The New American Right* (New York: Criterion, 1956); Bell, Daniel, "Passion and Politics in America," *Encounter* (November 1955); Birnbaum, Norman, "Monarchs and Sociologists: A Reply," *Sociological Review* (June 1955); Crossman, R. H. S., "On Political Neurosis," *Encounter* (May 1954); Duhl, Leonard, ed., *The Urban Condition* (New York: Basic Books, 1963); Gasset, Ortega Y., *The Revolt of The Masses* (New York: Norton, 1952); Goodman, Paul, *Growing Up Absurd* (New York: Random House, 1960); Greer, Scott, and Orleans, Peter, "Mass Society and the Parapolitical Structure," *American Sociological Review* (October 1962); Friedan, Betty, *The Feminine Mystique* (New York: Norton, 1963); Hoggart, Richard, *The Uses of Literacy* (London: Chatto & Windus, 1957); Horkheimer, Max, *Eclipse of Reason* (New York: Oxford University Press, 1947); Kitzinger, Uwe, "The Death of Ideology" *The Listener* (January 18, 1962); Kornhauser, William, *The Politics of Mass Society* (Glencoe, Ill.: Free Press, 1959); Lane, Robert, *Political Life* (Glencoe, Ill.: Free Press, 1959); Lazarsfeld,

Paul, "The Effects of Radio on Public Opinion," in *Print, Radio and Film in a Democracy* (Chicago: University of Chicago Press, 1942); Lederer, Emil, *The State of the Masses* (New York: Norton, 1940); Leggett, John, and Street, David, "Economic Deprivation and Extremism: A Study of Unemployed Negroes," *American Journal of Sociology* 67 (July 1961): 53–57; Leggett, John, and Street, David, "Uprootedness and Working-Class Consciousness," *American Journal of Sociology* (May 1963): 682–92; Leggett, John, and Street, David, "Economic Insecurity and Class Consciousness," *American Journal of Sociology* 29 (April, 1964: 227–34; Manis, Jerome, and Meltzer, Bernard, "Attitudes of Textile Workers to Class Structure," *American Journal of Sociology* 60 (July 1954): 30–55; Merton, Robert, et al.: *Reader in Bureaucracy* (Glencoe, Ill.: Free Press, 1952); Michels, Robert, *Political Parties* (New York: Hearst International Press, 1915); Rosenberg, Bernard, and White, David, eds., *Mass Culture* (Glencoe, Ill.: Free Press, 1957); Selznick, Phillip, *The Organizational Weapon* (New York: McGraw-Hill, 1952); Shils, Edward, "The End of Ideology?" *Encounter* (November 1955): 52–58; Shils, Edward, and Young, Michael, "The Meaning of the Coronation," *Sociological Review* (December 1953); Stouffer, Samuel, *Communism, Conformity and Civil Liberties* (Garden City, N.Y.: Doubleday, 1955); Swados, Harvey, *On the Line* (Boston: Little, Brown, 1957); Vidich, Arthur, and Bensmanm, Joseph, *Small Town in Mass Society* (Garden City, N.Y.: Doubleday, 1960).

The labor movement: Aronowitz, Stanley, "The Fate of the Unions," *Studies on the Left* (Spring 1964); Cochran, Bert, ed., *American Labor in Mid-Passage* (New York: Monthly Review, 1959); Hill, Herbert, "The ILGWU," *New Politics* 4, no. 1 (1962); Howe, Irving, and Widick, B. J., *The UAW and Walter Reuther* (New York: Random House, 1949); Kornhauser, Arthur, Sheppard, Harold, and Mayer, Albert, *When Labor Votes* (New York: University Books, 1956); Jacobs, Paul, *The State of the Unions* (New York: Atheneum, 1963); Lens, Sidney, *The Crisis of American Labor* (New York: Barnes, 1961); Lipset, Seymour, Trow, Martin, and Coleman, J. S., *Union Democracy* (Glencoe, Ill.: Free Press, 1956); Peck, Sidney, *The Rank-and-File Leader* (New Haven, Conn.: College and University Press, 1963); Perlman, S., *A Theory of the Labor Movement* (New York: Macmillan, 1928); Widick, B. J., *Labor Today* (Boston: Houghton, Mifflin, 1964).

On poverty in America: Conant, James, *Slums and Suburbs* (New York: Signet, 1961; Conference on Economic Progress, *Poverty and Deprivation in the United States* (Washington, D.C.: Author, 1962); Harrington, Michael, *The Other America* (New York: Macmillan, 1962); Hayden, Thomas, and Wittman, Carl, *An Interracial Movement of the Poor*? (New York: Students for a Democratic Society, 1964); Kuznets, Simon, *Shares of Upper Income Groups in Income and Savings* (New York: National Bureau of Economic Research, 1953); Lewis, Oscar, *The Children of Sanchez* (New York: Random House, 1961); Lewis, Oscar, *Five Families* (New York: Basic Books, 1959; Lewis, Oscar, *Pedro Martinez* (New York: Random House, 1964); Myrdal, Gunnar, *Challenge to Affluence* (New York: Pantheon, 1963); Schorr, Alvin, *Slums and Social Insecurity* (Washington, D.C.: U.S. Government Printing Office, 1963).

Civil rights: Baldwin, James, *The Fire Next Time* (New York: Dial, 1963); Baldwin, James, *Another Country* (New York: Dell, 1963); Drake, St. Clair, and Cayton, Horace, *Black Metropolis* (New York: Harper, 1945); Essien-Udom, E. U., *Black Nationalism* (Chicago: University of Chicago Press, 1962); Hayden, Thomas, *Revolution in Mississippi* (New York: Students for a Democratic Society, 1961); Hayden, Thomas, "Mission in McComb," *The Progressive* (December 1961); Hayden, Thomas, "The Negro Revolution in America," *International Socialist Review* (Winter 1963); Hayden, Thomas, "Liberal Analysis and Federal Power," *The Correspondent* (March–April 1964); Lomax, Louis, *The Negro Revolt* (New York: Signet, 1962); Lomax, Lewis, *When the Word Is Given* (New York: Signet, 1963); Lyton, David, *The Goddam White Man* (New York: Avon, 1960); Myrdal, Gunnar, *The American Dilemma* (New York:

Harper, 1944); Wakefield, Dan, *Revolt in the South* (New York: Grove, 1960); Wright, Richard, *Black Boy* (New York: Harper, 1937); Wright, Richard, *Native Son* (New York: Harper, 1937).

Sundry material on automation, employment, and the economics of defense and disarmament: Ad Hoc Committee, *The Triple Revolution* (Washington, D.C.: N.p., 1964); Allen, Donna, *The Economic Necessity to Disarm: A Challenge to the Old Assumptions*, paper given to Second International Arms Control and Disarmament Symposium, Ann Arbor, Michigan (January 23, 1964); Benoit, Emile, and Boulding, Kenneth, *Disarmament and the American Economy* (New York: Harper, 1963); Brand, Horst, "Disarmament and the Prospects for American Capitalism," *Dissent* (Summer 1962); Heilbroner, Robert, *The Future as History* (New York: Grove, 1959); Melman, Seymour, ed., *Disarmament: Its Politics and Economics* (New York: American Academy of Arts and Sciences, 1962); Melman, Seymour, *A Strategy for American Security* (New York: Lee Service, 1963); Michael, Donald, *Cybernation: The Silent Conquest* (Santa Barbara, Calif.: Fund for the Republic, 1962); U.S. Senate, Subcommittee on Employment and Manpower of the Committee on Labor and Public Welfare, *Exploring the Manpower Revolution*, Eighty-eighth Congress, Second Session (Washington, D.C.: U.S. Government Printing Office, 1964); U.S. Senate, *Toward Full Employment*, Eighty-eighth Congress, Second Session (Washington, D.C.: U.S. Government Printing Office, 1964).

The New Left and debates on "the young Marx," in America: Dunayevskaya, Raya, *Marxism and Freedom* (New York: Bookman, 1958); Feuer, Lewis, "What Is Alienation?" *New Politics* (Spring 1962): 116–34; Fromm, Erich, *Marx's Concept of Man* (New York: Ungar, 1961); Harrington, Michael, "Marx versus Marx," *New Politics* (Fall 1961); Lichteim, George, *Marxism* (Boston: Praeger, 1961). In England: MacKenzie, Norman, ed., *Conviction* (New York: Monthly Review, 1959); Thompson, E. P., ed., *Out of Apathy* (London: Stevens & Sons, 1960); Taylor, Charles, "Alienation and Community," *Universities and Left Review* 5 (Autumn 1958); Thompson, E. P., "Socialist Humanism," *New Reasoner* (Summer 1957); Thompson, E. P., "Socialism and the Intellectuals," *Universities and Left Review* (Spring 1957). In France: Calvez, J. Y., *La Pensée de Karl Marx* (Paris: N.p., 1956); Fougeyrolles, Pierre, "De Marx à Nous," *Arguments* (January–February–March 1959); Goldmann, Lucien, "La Reification," *Les Temps Modernes* (February–March 1959); Guerin, Daniel, "De Jeune Marx à Marx," *Arguments* (January–February–March 1959); Sartre, Jean-Paul, *La Critique de la Raison Dialectique* (Paris: N.p., 1960); Sartre, Jean-Paul, "Le Fantome de Staline," *Les Temps Modernes* (November–December 1956, January 1957). In Germany: Fetscher, Irving, ed., *Marximus-Studien*, 3 vols. (Tübingen: N.p., 1954, 1957, 1960). In general: Hayden, Thomas, "The Young Marx and the New Revisionism," unpublished paper (Ann Arbor, 1963); Kolakowski, Leszek, "The Priest and the Jester," *Dissent* (Summer 1962); Kolakowski, Leszek, "The Conspiracy of the Ivory Tower Intellectuals," in *Marxism* (New York: Bantam, 1961); Labedz, L., ed., *Revisionism* (London: Allen & Unwin, 1962); Schaff, Adam, *A Philosophy of Man* (New York: Monthly Review, 1963).

Socialism and Communism in America: Draper, Theodore, *The Roots of American Communism* (New York: Viking, 1957); Draper, Theodore, *American Communism and Soviet Russia* (New York: Viking, 1960); Egbert, Donald, et al., *Socialism and American Life* (Princeton, N.J.: Princeton University Press, 1952); Fleischmann, Harry, *Norman Thomas* (New York: Norton, 1964); Howe, Irving, and Coser, Lewis, *The American Communist Party* (Boston: Beacon, 1951); Shannon, David, *The Socialist Party of America* (New York: Macmillan, 1955); Weinstein, James, "Socialism's Hidden Heritage," *Studies of the Left* 3, no. 4 (Fall 1963).

Other commentary on liberalism and radicalism: de Beauvoir, Simone, *The Mandarins* (New York: World, 1956); Editors of *Dissent, Voices of Dissent* (New York: Grove, 1954); Hagan, Roger, "Between Two Eras," *The Correspondent* (April–May

1964); Hayden, Thomas, "Who Are the Student Boatrockers?" *Mademoiselle* (September 1961); Hayden, Thomas, "Contra: In Loco Parentis," *Dissent* (Winter 1964): Hayden, Thomas, *Student Social Action* (New York: Students for a Democratic Society, 1961); Howe, Irving, *A World More Attractive* (New York: N.p., 1964); Lessing, Doris, *The Golden Notebook* (New York: Simon & Schuster, 1962); Lynd, Staughton, "Socialism: The Forbidden Word," *Studies on the Left* (Winter 1964); Kempton, Murray, *America Comes of Middle-Age* (New York: Little, Brown, 1963); MacDonald, Dwight, *Memoirs of a Revolutionist* (New York: Farrar, Strauss, & Cudahy, 1962); Orwell, George, *Homage to Catalona* (Boston: Beacon, 1952); Roosevelt, James, ed., *The Liberal Papers* (Garden City, N.Y.: Anchor, 1962); Sigel, Clancy, *Going Away* (New York: Houghton, Mifflin, 1962); Swados, Harvey, *A Radical's America* (New York: World, 1962); Stone, I. F., *The Haunted Fifties* (New York: Random House, 1963).

Index

213

About the Author and Contributors

Tom Hayden, former California state senator, has been a nationally influential activist since his co-founding of Students for a Democratic Society in the 1960s. He lives in Los Angeles and has taught at Occidental and Pitzer Colleges. Among his many books are *Street Wars: Gangs and the Future of Violence* (2004) and *The Port Huron Statement: The Visionary Call of the 1960s Revolution* (2005).

Dick Flacks is professor of sociology at the University of California Santa Barbara and is also one of the founders of Students for a Democratic Society along with Tom Hayden during the 1960s. He is author of *Making History: The American Left and the American Mind* (1988).

Stanley Aronowitz is professor of sociology and cultural studies at the Graduate Center of the City University of New York and the author of *How Class Works* (Yale University Press 2003). He was also a colleague of Tom Hayden during the 1960s.

Charles Lemert is Andrus Professor of Sociology at Wesleyan University and the author recently of *Durkheim's Ghosts* (Cambridge University Press 2005) and *Postmodernism Is Not What You Think*, Second Edition (Paradigm 2005.